THE MANN-WEIL SONGBOOK

PIANO
VOCAL
GUITAR

Photo by William "PoPsie" Randolph
www.PoPsiePhotos.com

ISBN 1-4234-0688-5

HAL•LEONARD®
CORPORATION
7777 W. BLUEMOUND RD. P.O. BOX 13819 MILWAUKEE, WI 53213

Visit Hal Leonard Online at
www.halleonard.com

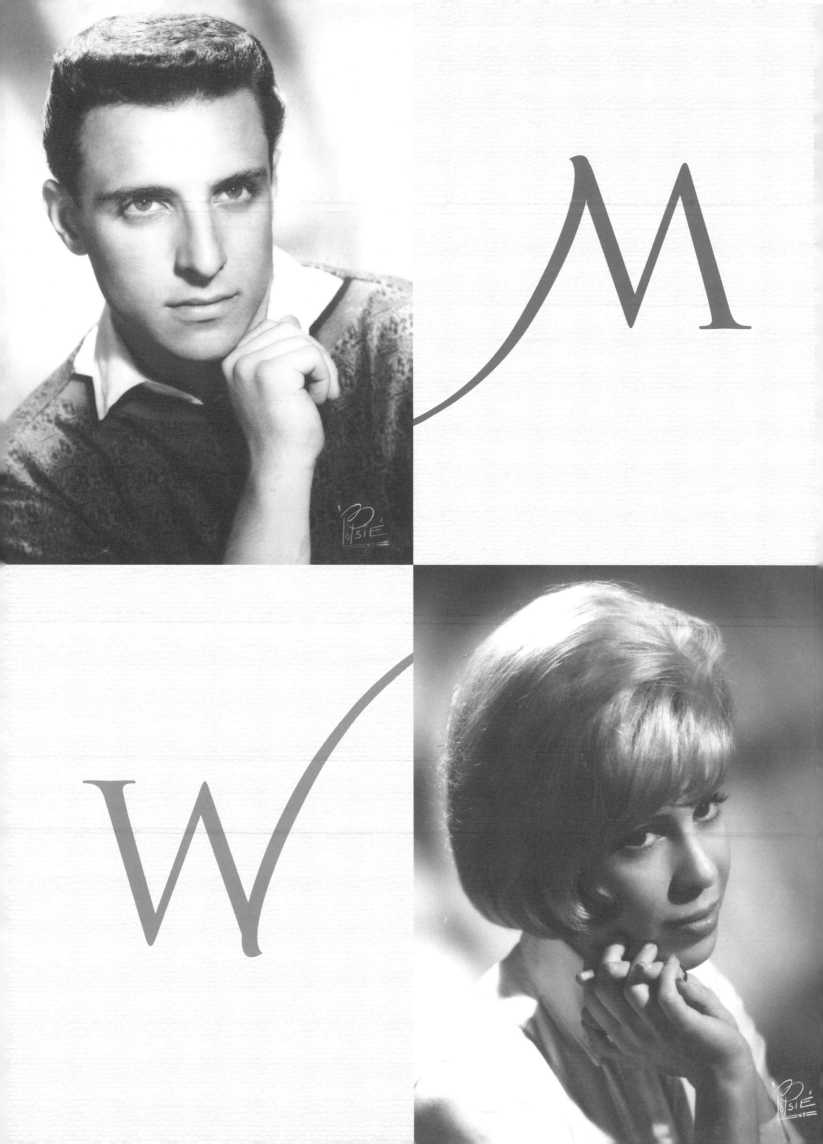

BARRY MANN
CYNTHIA WEIL

It would be impossible to imagine the last four decades of pop music without the melodies of Barry Mann and the lyrics of Cynthia Weil. One of the most successful pure songwriting teams in history, Mann and Weil have created a body of work so significant it has often been described as "a soundtrack to our lives."

Together, this husband and wife team have written songs like "You've Lost That Lovin' Feeling" (with Phil Spector), "On Broadway" (with Jerry Lieber and Mike Stoller), "Walking in the Rain," "Kicks," "Soul and Inspiration," "We Gotta Get Out of This Place," "I Just Can't Help Believing," "Here You Come Again," "Never Gonna Let You Go," "Just Once," and the GRAMMY® nominated "Don't Know Much" (with Tom Snow) to name a few. The list of their chart hits spans the decades from the sixties through the nineties.

However, no mere list can describe how influential their work has been. Early Mann/Weil successes like "He's Sure the Boy I Love," "Blame It on the Bossa Nova" and "Walking in the Rain" established them as writers with the ability to create catchy songs. But soon they were producing words and music that had an impact far beyond that of the average hit.

"You've Lost That Lovin' Feeling" and "Soul and Inspiration" were not just songs that launched The Righteous Brothers, they defined the genre we call "blue-eyed soul". "On Broadway," "Uptown" and "Only in America" transcended early rock and roll's romantic "moon and June" fixation. "Kicks" proved that Mann and Weil, unlike many of their contemporaries, could not only write for rock bands but that a commercial hit could address a serious issue like drugs. "We Gotta Get Out of This Place" is not only considered one of the classic rock songs of all time, but it became an anthem for Vietnam soldiers and protesters alike.

"Here You Come Again" provided country star Dolly Parton with her first crossover hit and helped country artists take their rightful place in the world of popular music. "Just Once" launched the career of a great emotional vocalist named James Ingram and the soulful "Don't Know Much" reintroduced the world to the angelic voice of Aaron Neville.

Mann and Weil began their careers in the '60s at Aldon Music, the legendary music publishing company founded by Don Kirshner and Al Nevins. They were members of a teen writing staff, which included Carole King and Gerry Goffin, Neil Sedaka and Howard Greenfield and Carole Bayer Sager. Among their other Brill Building colleagues were the likes of Jeff Barry, Ellie Greenwich, Jerry Lieber, Mike Stoller and Phil Spector.

Throughout their collaboration, Barry and Cynthia have worked with other writers. Cynthia wrote the lyrics to "Running with the Night" with Lionel Richie, "He's So Shy" with Tom Snow, "If Ever You're in My Arms Again" with Snow and Michael Masser, the GRAMMY nominated "Through the Fire" with David Foster and Tom Keane, and "Wrong Again" with Tommy Lee James. In 1999 "Wrong Again," recorded by Martina McBride, hit #1 on the country charts.

Barry was both co-writer, with Gerry Goffin, and recording artist on "Who Put the Bomp" and he co-wrote "I Love How You Love Me" with Larry Kolber, "How Much Love" with Leo Sayer and "Sometimes When We Touch" with Dan Hill.

In addition to countless appearances of their classics onscreen, Mann and Weil have created song scores for such films as *An American Tail* for which they wrote the double GRAMMY-winning "Somewhere Out There" with James Horner. In addition to collecting GRAMMYs for "Song of the Year" and "Motion Picture or Television Song of the Year", the song also won Golden Globe and Oscar nominations, BMI's Most Performed Film Song

Award and became an instant standard. Other films in which Mann/Weil original songs have appeared include *About Last Night, National Lampoon's Christmas Vacation, Oliver and Company* and *Balto*. "Whatever You Imagine" from *The Pagemaster* won Mann and Weil another GRAMMY nomination for "Motion Picture or Television Song of the Year" in 1995. One of their favorite song scores is the one they wrote for *Muppet Treasure Island*.

Cynthia collaborated with John Williams on the theme for Steven Spielberg's *A.I.* "For Always," recorded by Josh Groban, appeared on the film's soundtrack CD. In 2004 Weil wrote "Remember" with James Horner for the film *Troy*. "Remember" was nominated for a World Soundtrack Award for "Best Song Written Directly for a Film."

Barry and Cynthia have amassed an incredible 107 pop, country and R&B awards from Broadcast Music Inc., recognizing highest performance popularity on American radio and television in a particular year and 91 Millionaire awards, signifying radio performances of a million or more plays.

"You've Lost That Lovin' Feeling" has been honored as the most performed song in the BMI catalogue and the most performed song of the twentieth century. It has garnered more than eleven million performances, the first BMI song ever to achieve that milestone. If played back-to-back 24 hours a day, this equals more than 63 years of continuous airplay. The rock and roll classic has also received 14 pop awards...another record achievement, and The Righteous Brothers' recording has been selected for inclusion in the GRAMMY Hall of Fame.

Additional recognition of Mann and Weil's achievements include: the first Lifetime Achievement Award from the National Academy of Songwriters; The Clooney Foundation's Award for Legendary Song Composition; BMI's Robert Burton Award for the most performed country song of 1977, "Here You Come Again"; induction into the prestigious Songwriters Hall of Fame; and the 2003 Heroes Award from the New York Chapter of NARAS.

In January 2004, Mann and Weil opened in New York for a limited run of *They Wrote That?*, a show based on their catalogue of hit songs. Backed by a five piece band and three back up singers, Barry sang while Cynthia wove their personal and professional history, stories about the creative process and behind the scenes dish, through an evening of their songs. The show was directed by Tony® Award-winning director, Richard Maltby, Jr.

Mann and Weil are currently working on an original pop rock musical based on the motion picture classic, *Mask*, also to be directed by Maltby. Anna Hamilton Phelan, screenwriter of the film has written the *Mask* book for the theatrical version.

In recent years Barry has also made his mark in the world of photography. He has had three exhibits in Los Angeles and is preparing for a fourth in April 2006.

For additional Mann-Weil information visit their website at Mann-Weil.com.

BLAME IT ON THE BOSSA NOVA

Words and Music by BARRY MANN
and CYNTHIA WEIL

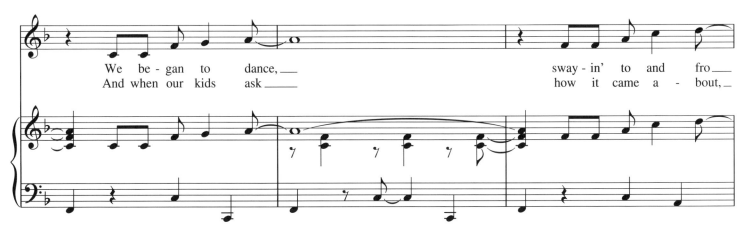

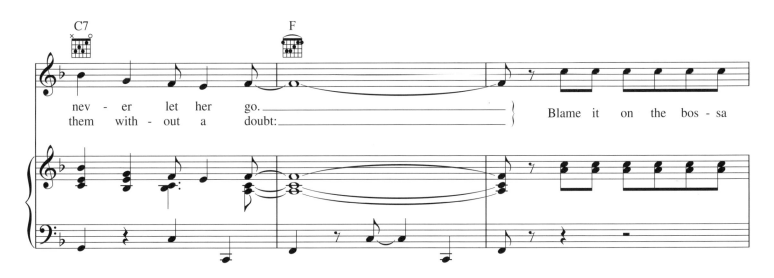

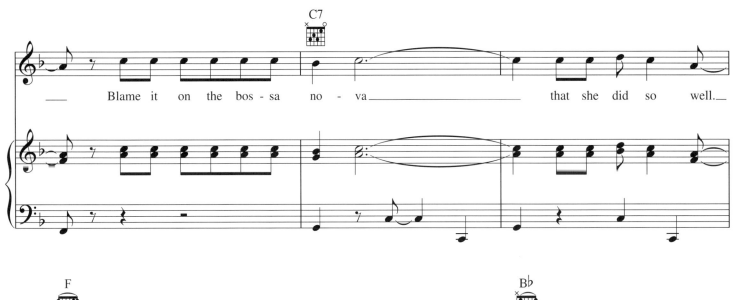

Blame it on the bos - sa no - va _____ that she did so well. __

_____ Oh, it all be - gan with just one lit - tle dance, __

__ but soon it end - ed up a big ro - mance. __ Blame it on the bos - sa

no - va, _____ the dance of love. _____

DON'T KNOW MUCH

Words and Music by BARRY MANN,
CYNTHIA WEIL and TOM SNOW

Tenderly

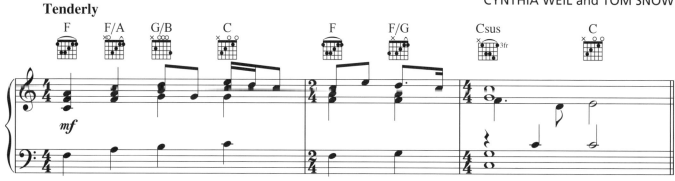

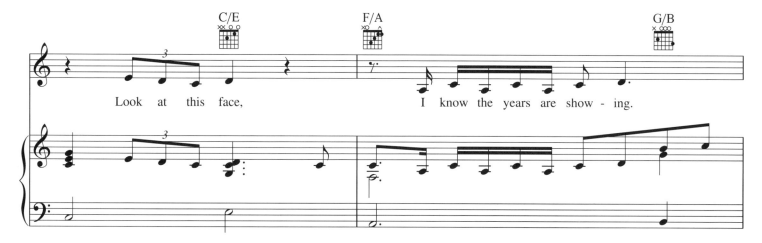

Look at this face, I know the years are show - ing.

Look at this life, _____ I still don't know where _ it's go - ing.

I don't know _____ much, but I know I love you, _____ and

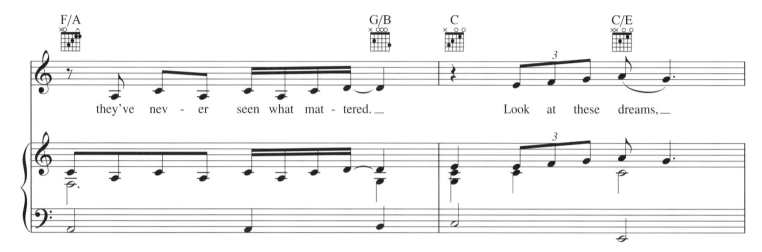

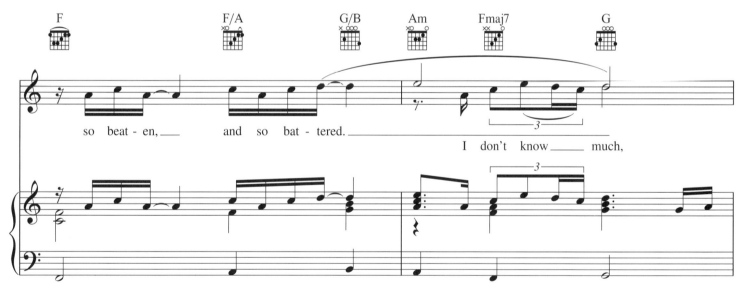

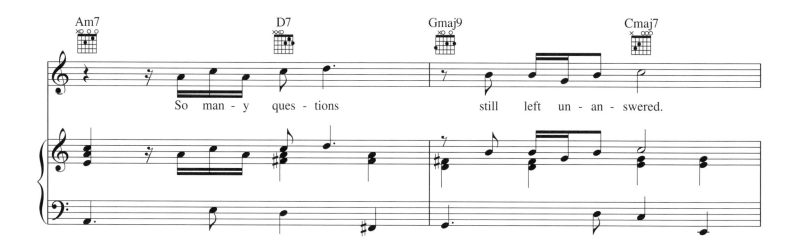

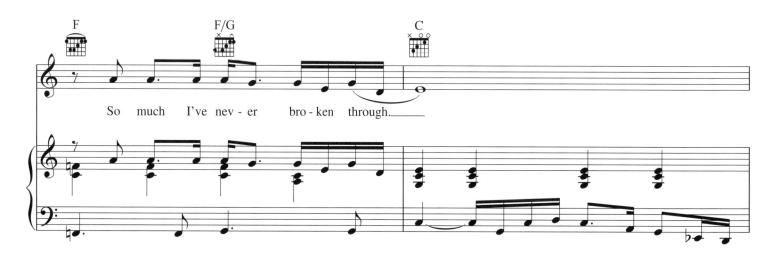

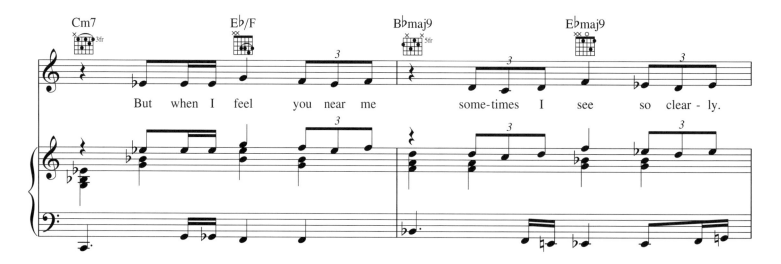

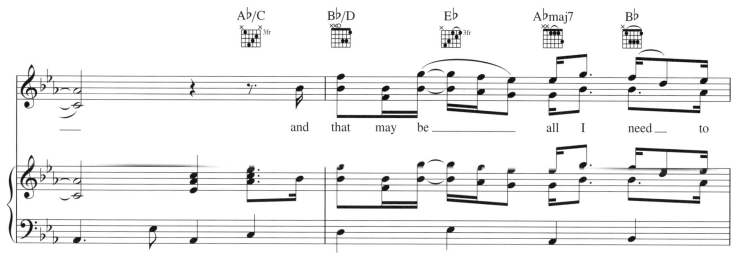

and that may be _____ all I need ___ to

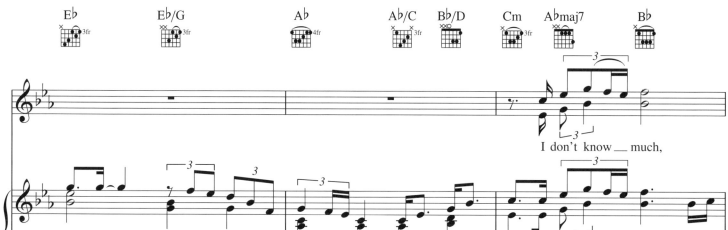

know.

I don't know ___ much,

but I know I love you, _____ and

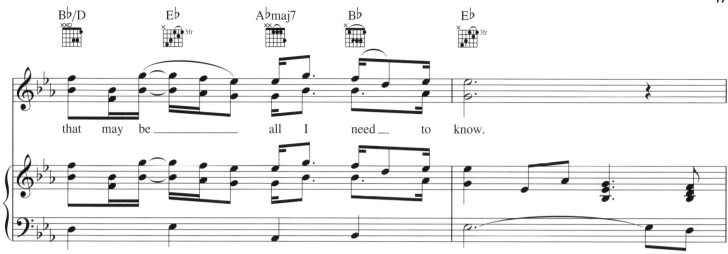

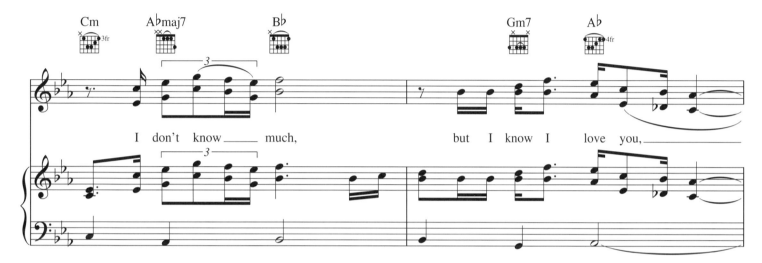

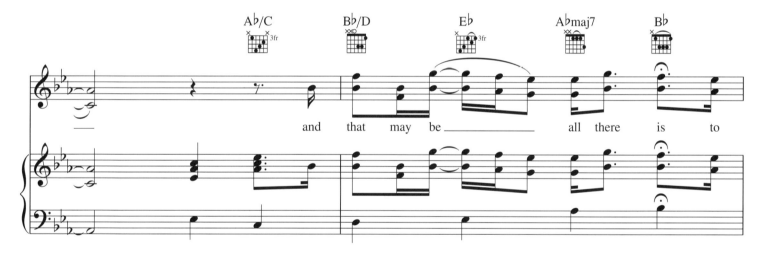

HE'S SO SHY

Words and Music by CYNTHIA WEIL
and TOM SNOW

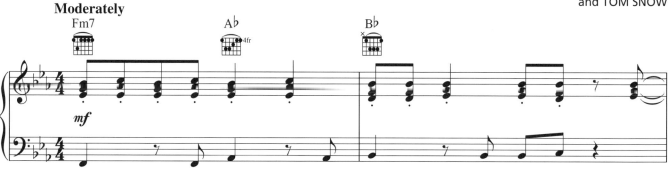

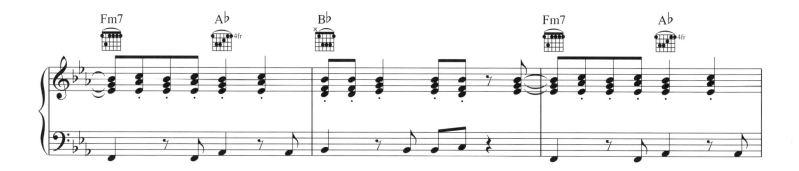

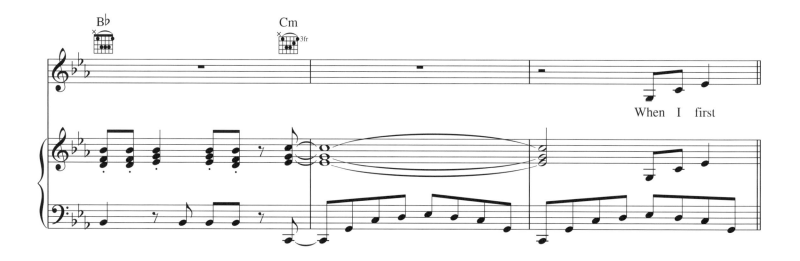

When I first

saw him stand-ing there, __ I longed to speak __ but did __ not dare.

gen-tly through __ the night, __ noth-ing has ev- er felt __ so right. __

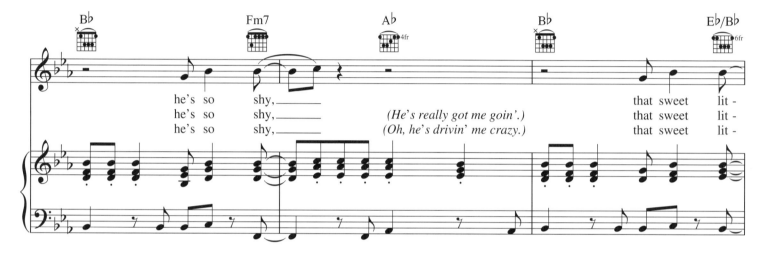

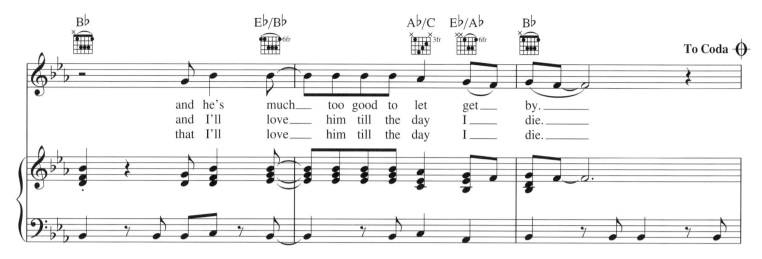

To Coda ⊕

and he's much___ too good to let get___ by.___
and I'll love___ him till the day I ___ die.___
that I'll love___ him till the day I ___ die.___

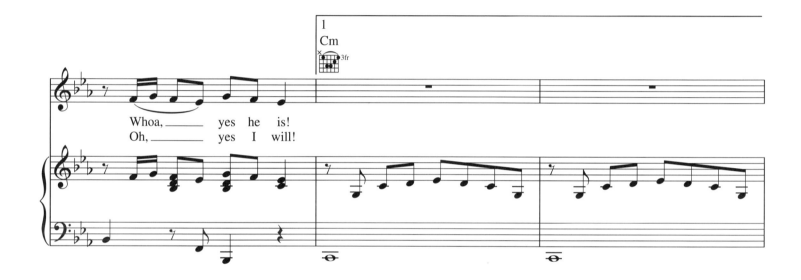

Whoa,_____ yes he is!
Oh,_____ yes I will!

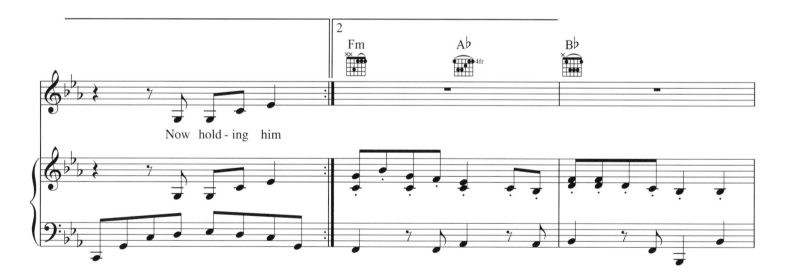

Now hold - ing him

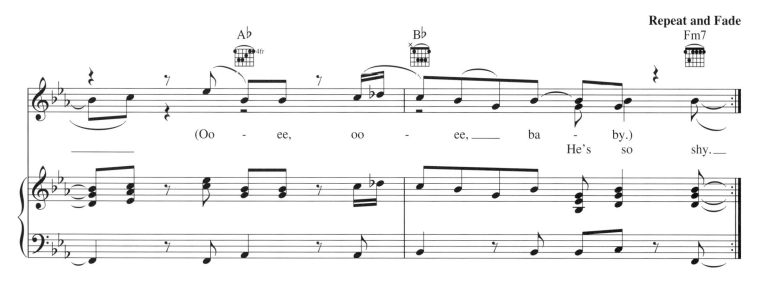

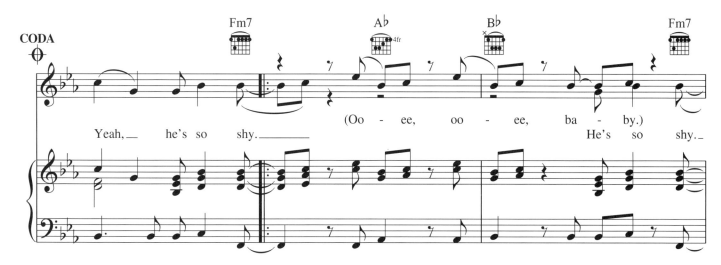

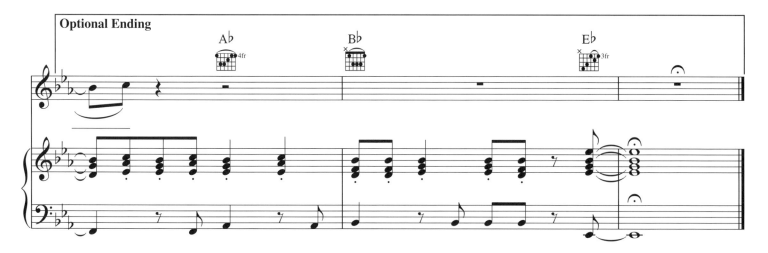

HERE YOU COME AGAIN

Words by CYNTHIA WEIL
Music by BARRY MANN

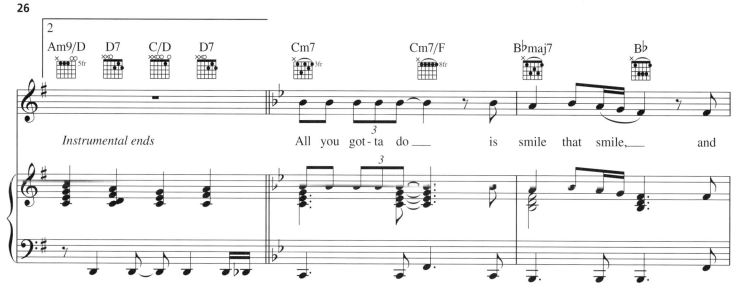

Instrumental ends

All you got-ta do ___ is smile that smile, ___ and

there go all ___ my ___ de - fens - es. ___ Just

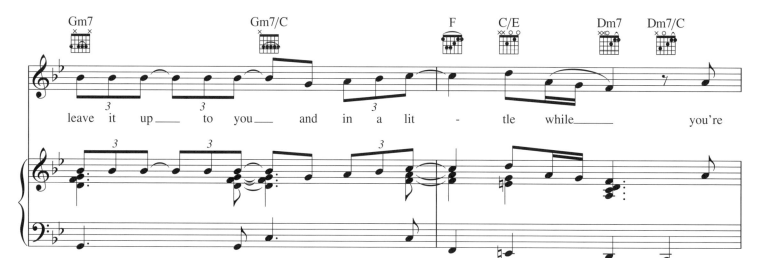

leave it up ___ to you ___ and in a lit - tle while ___ you're

mess - in' up ___ my mind ___ and fill - in' up ___ my sens - es.

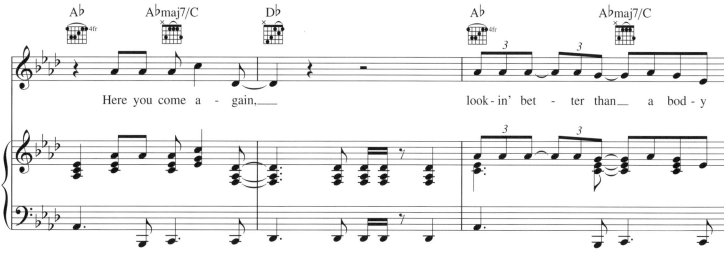

Here you come a - gain,___ look-in' bet - ter than___ a bod - y

has a right___ to, and shak - in' me___ up so that all I real - ly know is

here you come___ a - gain___ and here I_____ go._____

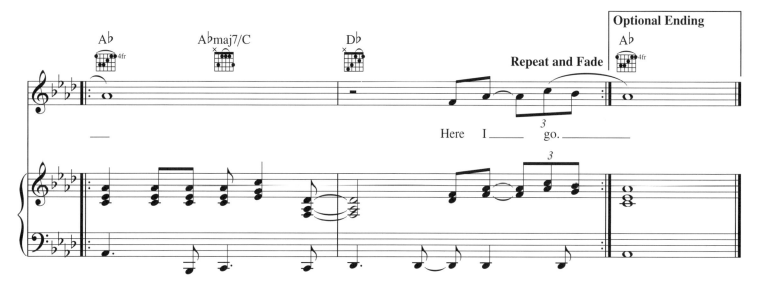

Here I_____ go._____

HE'S SURE THE BOY I LOVE

Words and Music by BARRY MANN
and CYNTHIA WEIL

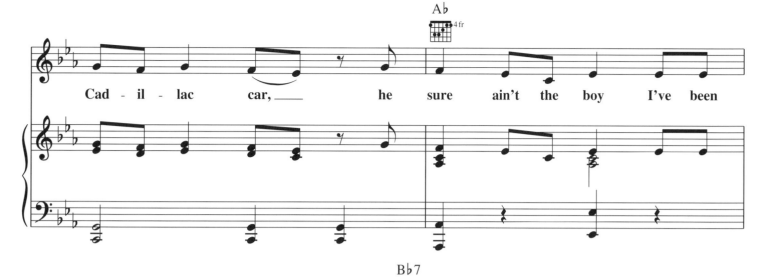

Cad - il - lac car, ____ he sure ain't the boy I've been

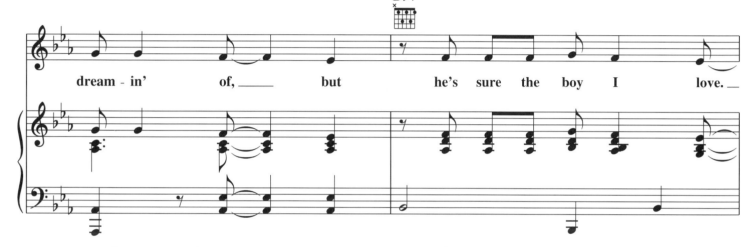

dream - in' of, ____ but he's sure the boy I love. ____

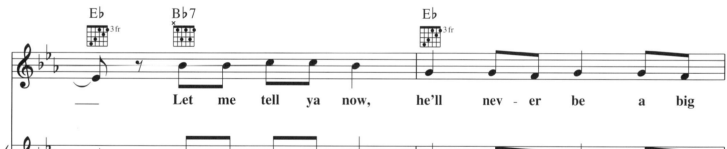

____ Let me tell ya now, he'll nev - er be a big

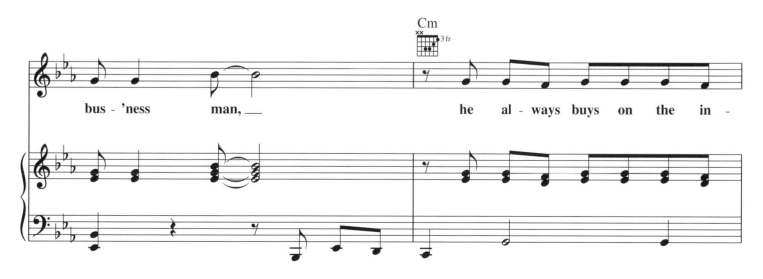

bus - 'ness man, ____ he al - ways buys on the in -

stall - ment plan, ___ he sure ain't the boy I've been

dream - in' of, ___ but he's sure the boy I love. ___

___ When he holds me tight, ___ ev - 'ry-thing's right, ___

cra - zy as it seems. ___ I'm his, what -

HUNGRY

Words and Music by BARRY MANN
and CYNTHIA WEIL

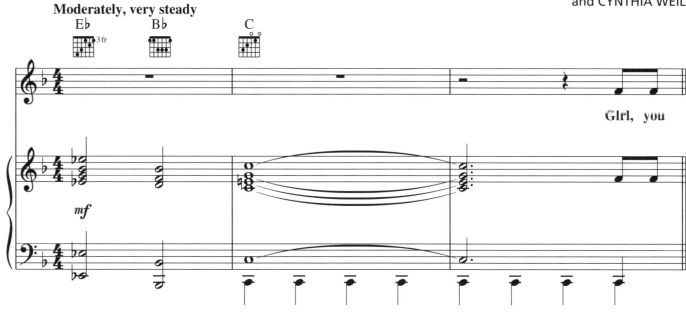

Girl, you

got this need to know what I'm all a - bout. ___
cus - tom tai - lored world that I've got - ta own ___

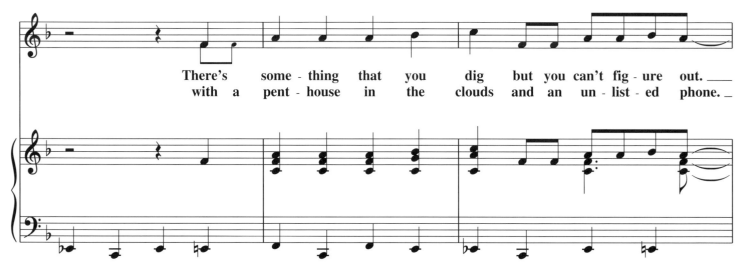

There's some - thing that you dig but you can't fig - ure out. ___
with a pent - house in the clouds and an un - list - ed phone. __

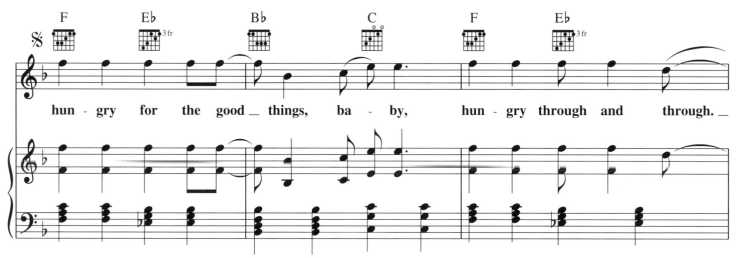

hun - gry for the good _ things, ba - by, hun - gry through and through. _

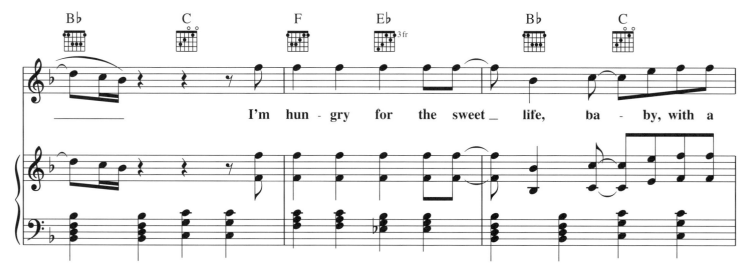

_ I'm hun - gry for the sweet _ life, ba - by, with a

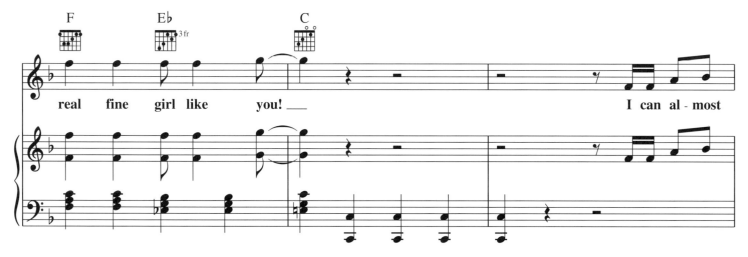

real fine girl like you! _ I can al - most

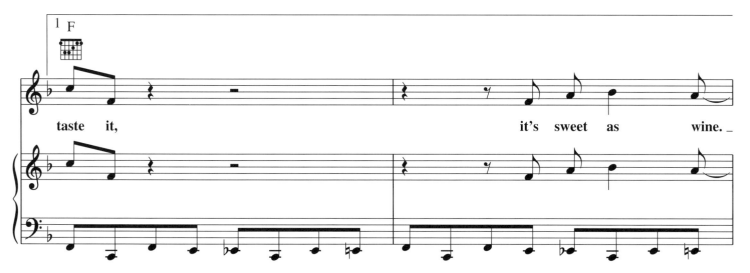

taste it, it's sweet as wine. _

I JUST CAN'T HELP BELIEVIN'

Words and Music by BARRY MANN
and CYNTHIA WEIL

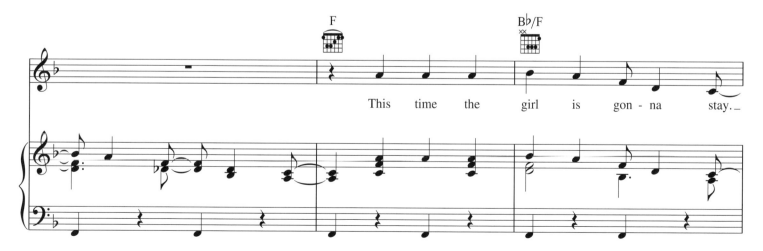

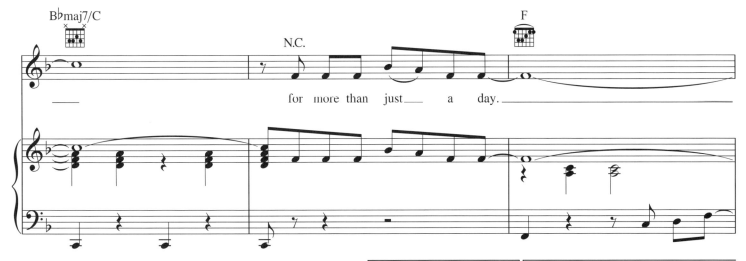

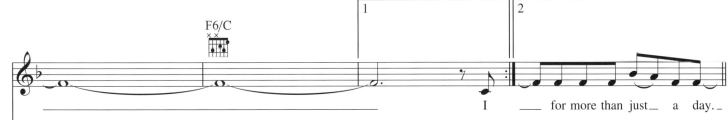

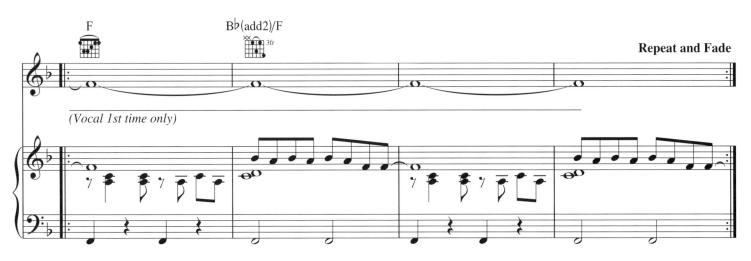

(Vocal 1st time only)

IF EVER YOU'RE IN MY ARMS AGAIN

Words and Music by MICHAEL MASSER,
TOM SNOW and CYNTHIA WEIL

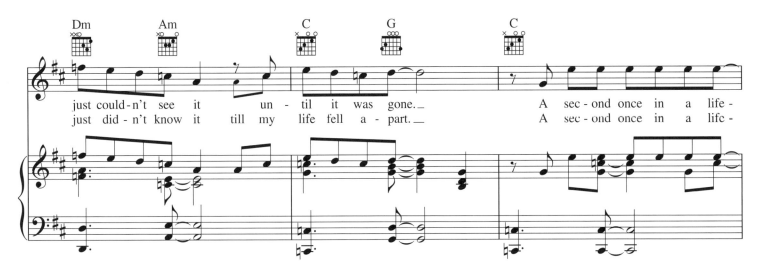

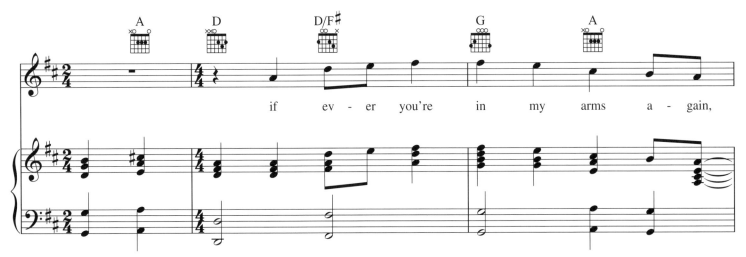

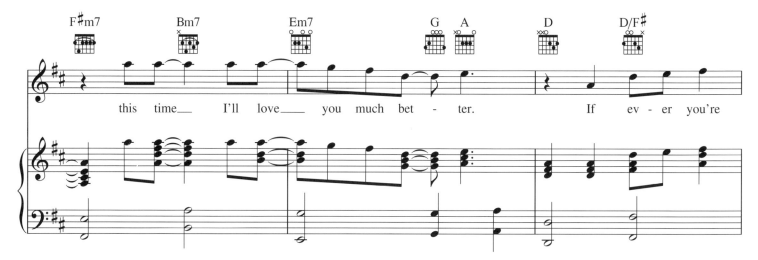

this time___ I'll love___ you much bet - ter. If ev - er you're

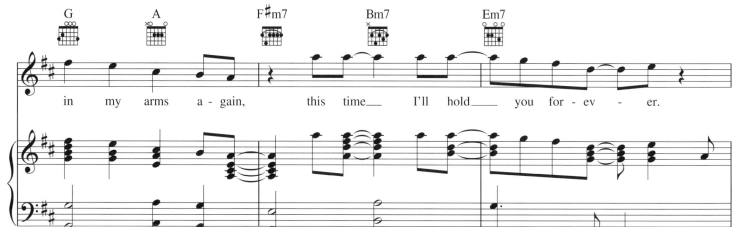

in my arms a - gain, this time___ I'll hold___ you for - ev - er.

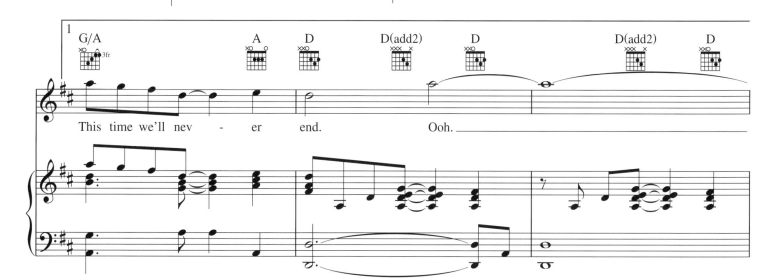

This time we'll nev - er end. Ooh. ___

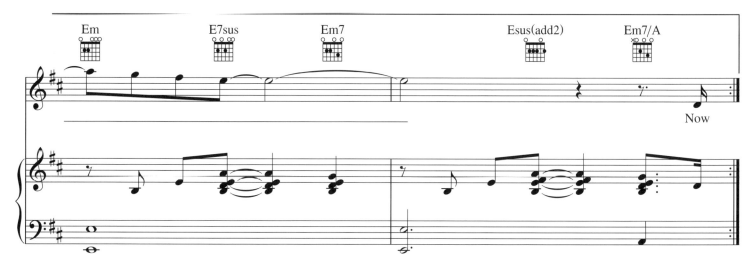

Now

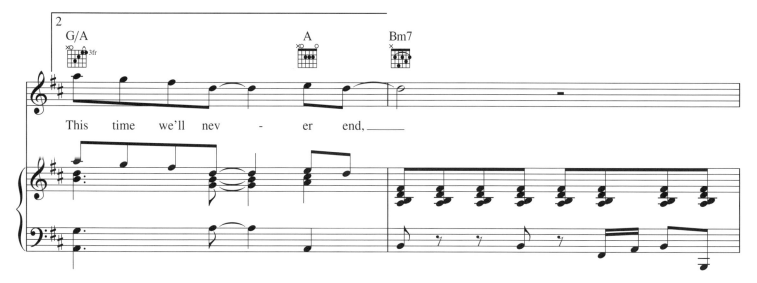

This time we'll nev - er end, _____

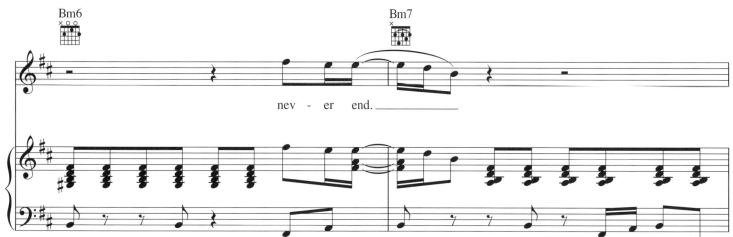

nev - er end. _____

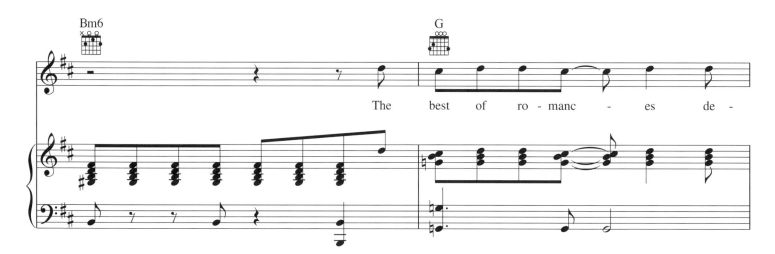

The best of ro - manc - es de -

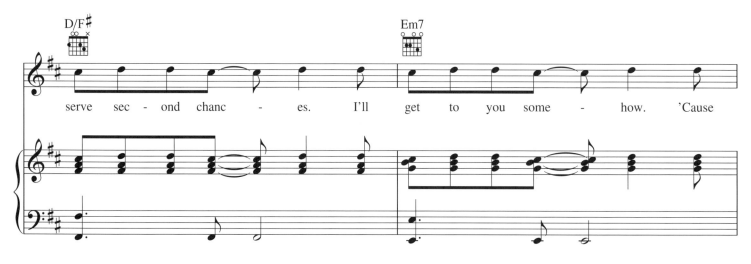

serve sec - ond chanc - es. I'll get to you some - how. 'Cause

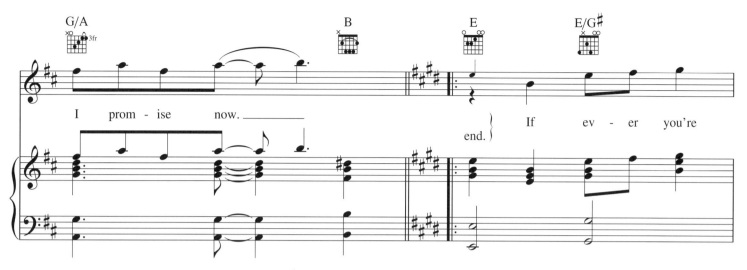

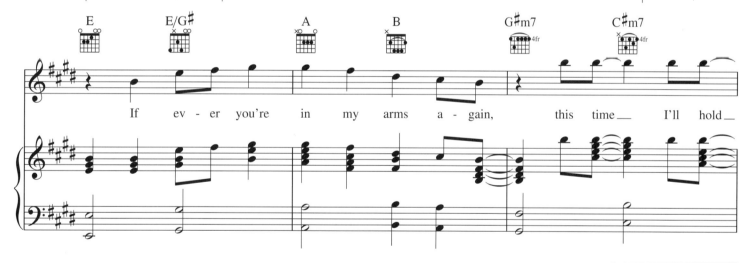

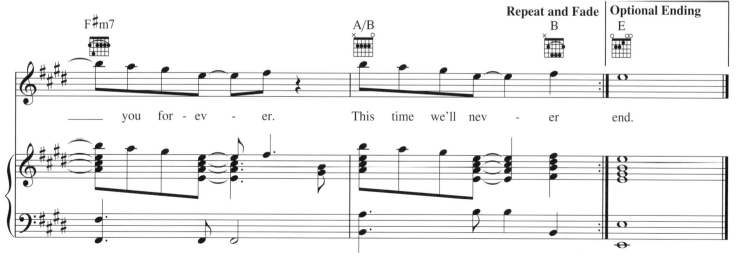

JUST ONCE

Words by CYNTHIA WEIL
Music by BARRY MANN

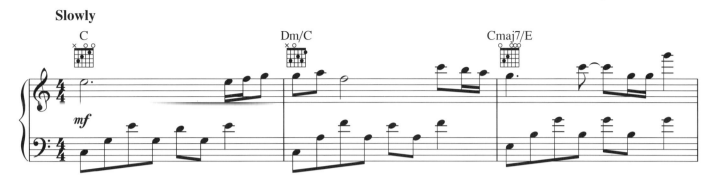

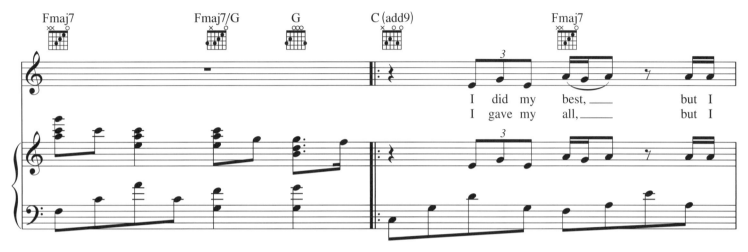

I did my best, ____ but I
I gave my all, ____ but I

guess my best was-n't good ___ e-nough ___ 'cause here we are, ___ back ___ where we were ___ be-fore. ___
think my all ___ may have been ___ too much ___ 'cause Lord knows we're ___ not ___ get-ting an - y - where. ___

Seems noth-ing ev - er chang - es, we're
It seems we're al - ways blow - in' what-

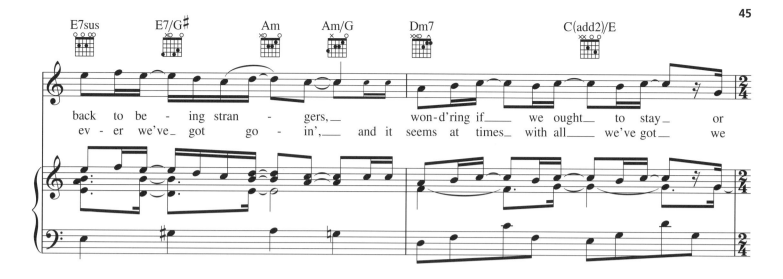

back to be - ing stran - gers, _ won-d'ring if _ we ought _ to stay _ or
ev - er we've _ got go - in', _ and it seems at times _ with all _ we've got _ we

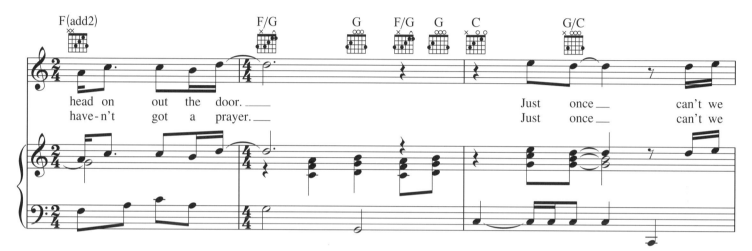

head on out the door. _
have-n't got a prayer. _
Just once _ can't we
Just once _ can't we

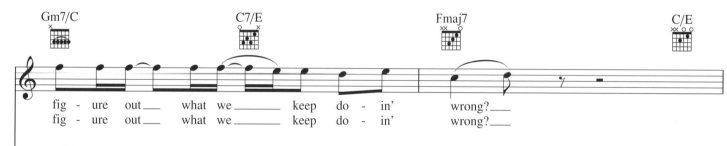

fig - ure out _ what we _____ keep do - in' wrong? _
fig - ure out _ what we _____ keep do - in' wrong? _

Why we nev - er last _ for ver - y long? _
Why the good _ times nev - er last _ for long? _
What are we do -
Where are we go -

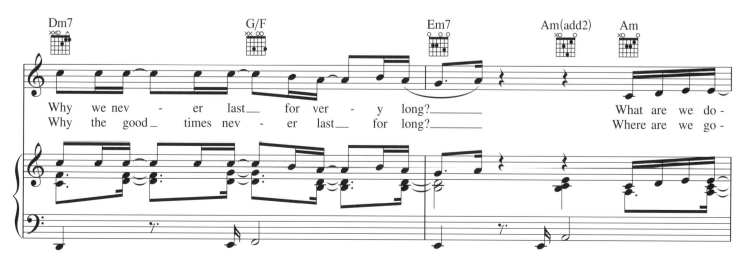

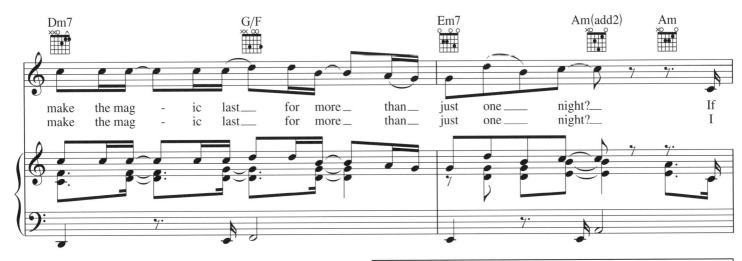

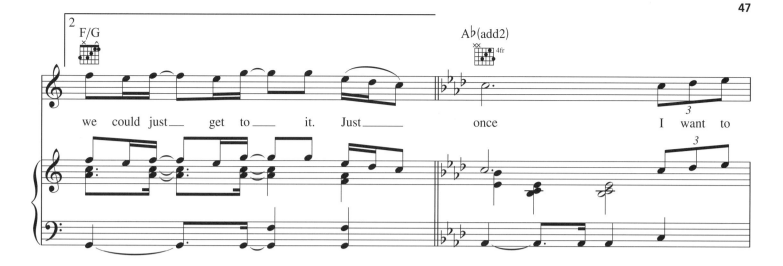

we could just___ get to___ it. Just___ once I want to

un-der-stand_____ why it al-ways_ comes back__ to good-

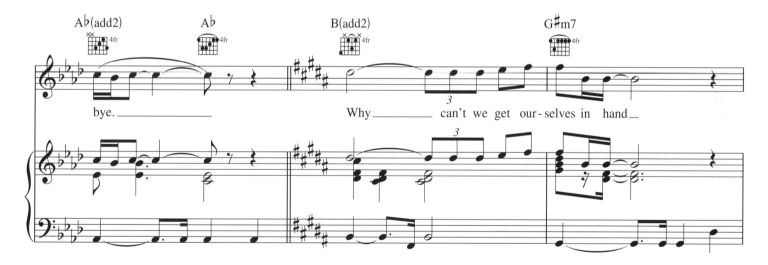

bye._____ Why_____ can't we get our-selves in hand_

and ad-mit to one__ an-oth___-er we're no good with-out__ each oth___-er,

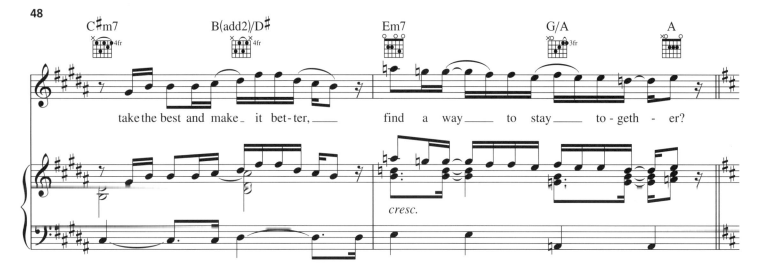

take the best and make_ it bet-ter,____ find a way____ to stay____ to-geth -er?

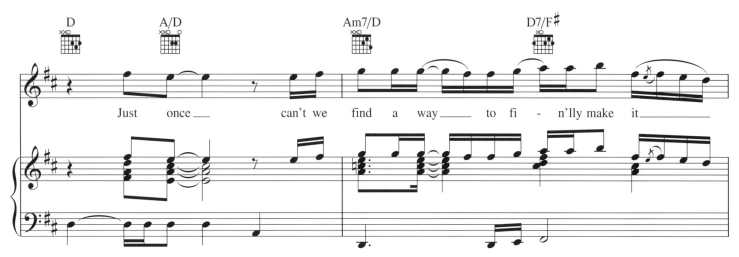

Just once___ can't we find a way____ to fi - n'lly make it_____

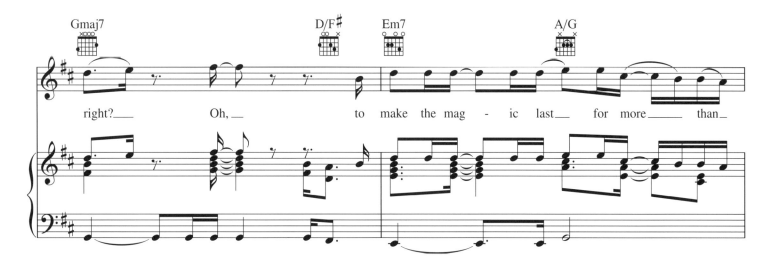

right?____ Oh, ___ to make the mag - ic last___ for more____ than_

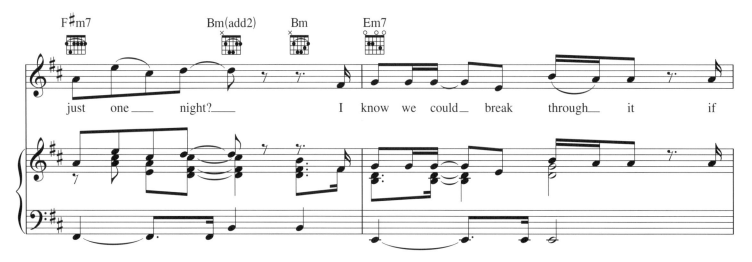

just one ___ night?____ I know we could_ break through___ it if

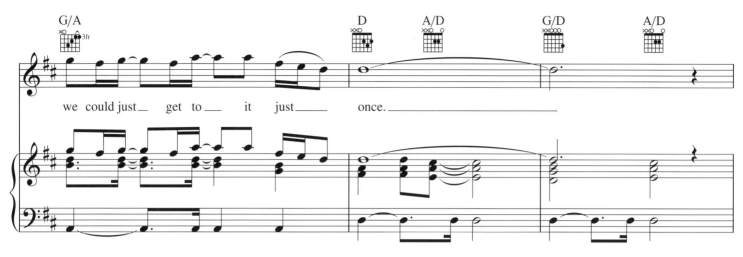

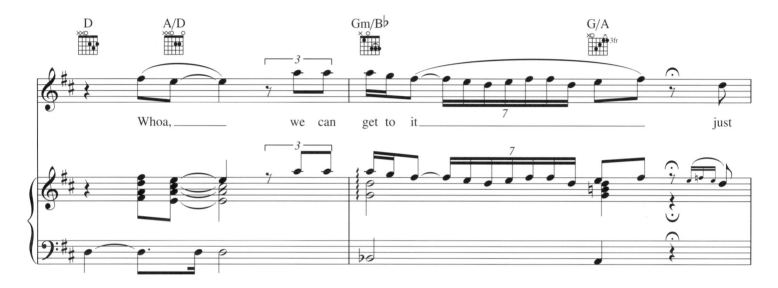

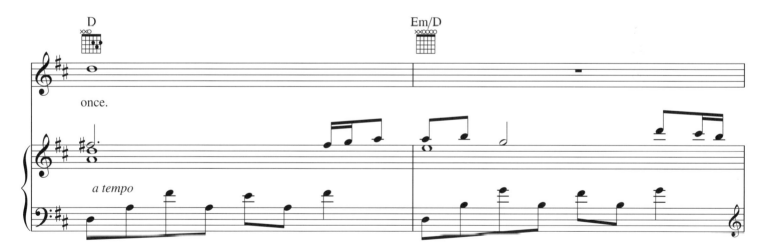

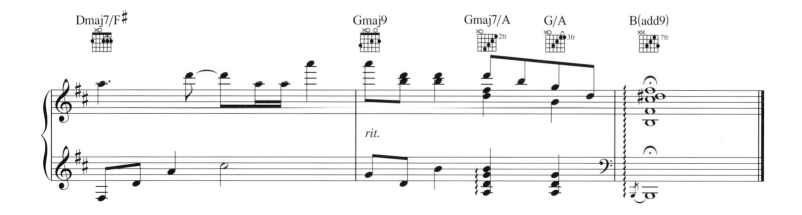

KICKS

Words and Music by BARRY MANN
and CYNTHIA WEIL

Girl, you thought you found the an - swer on that
think you're gon - na find your - self a

mag - ic car - pet ride last night.
lit - tle piece of par - a - dise.

But when you wake up in the morn - in', the world
But it ain't hap - pened yet, so, girl,

52

SOMETIMES WHEN WE TOUCH

Words by DAN HILL
Music by BARRY MANN

rather hurt_____ you hon - est - ly_____ than mis-
through the in - se - cu - ri - ty_____ some
watched while love_____ com - mands_____ you,_____ and I've

lead you with_____ a lie. And who am I_____ to judge_____
ten - der - ness_____ sur - vives. I'm just an - oth - er writ -
watched love pass_____ you by. At times I think_____ we're drift -

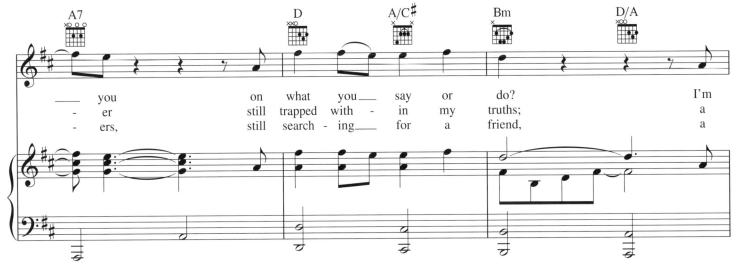

_____ you on what you_____ say or do? I'm a
- er still trapped with - in my truths; a
- ers, still search - ing_____ for a friend, a

on - ly just_____ be - gin - ning to see the real_____ you.
hes - i - tant_____ prize-fight - er still trapped with - in_____ my youth.
broth - er or_____ a sis - ter, but then the pas - sion flares_____ a - gain.

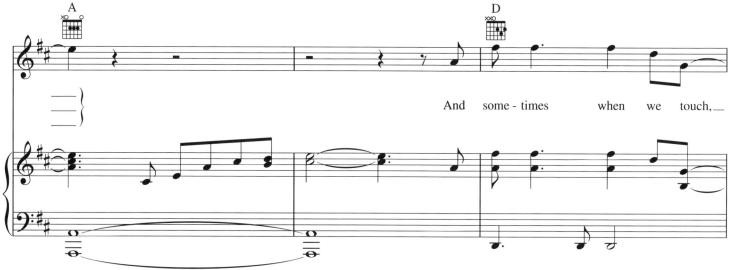

And some - times when we touch,___

___ the hon - es - ty's___ too ___ much.___ And I

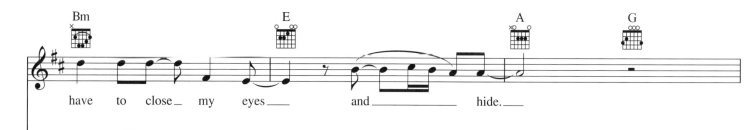

have to close___ my eyes ___ and _____ hide.___

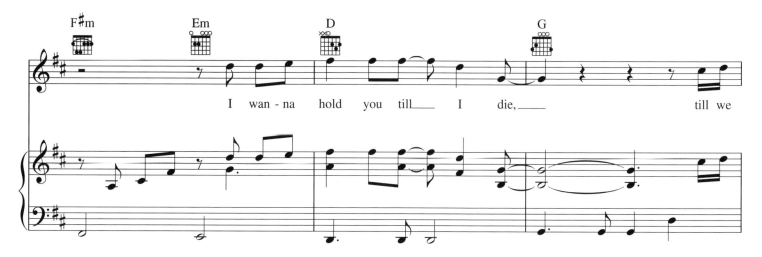

I wan - na hold you till___ I die,___ till we

both break down _____ and cry. _____ I wan-na hold you till the fear _____

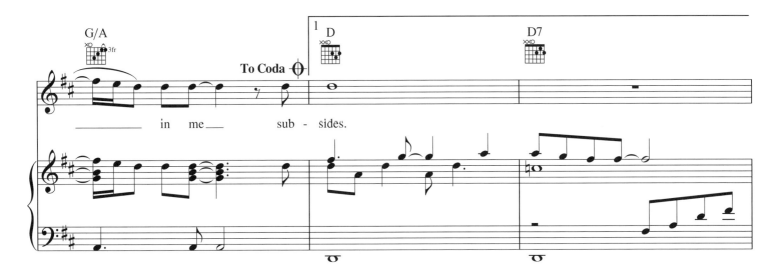

_____ in me _____ sub - sides.

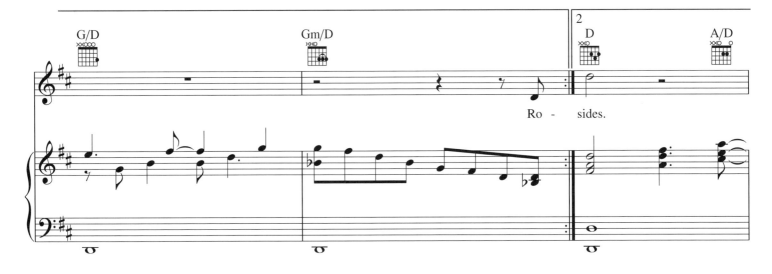

Ro - sides.

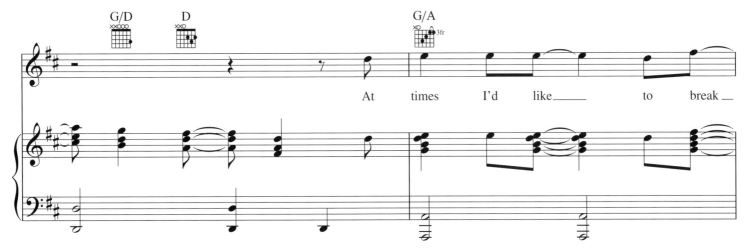

At times I'd like _____ to break _____

you and drive you to your knees. At

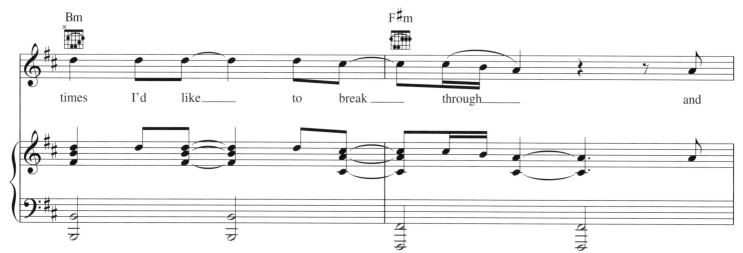

times I'd like to break through and

hold you end - less - ly. At

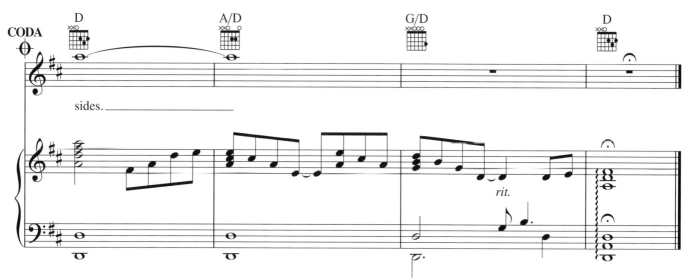

sides.

MAKE YOUR OWN KIND OF MUSIC

Words and Music by BARRY MANN
and CYNTHIA WEIL

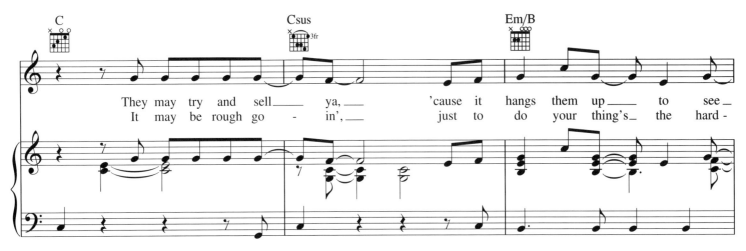

_____ some - one _____ like you. _____)
- est thing _____ to _____ do. _____)

But you've got - ta

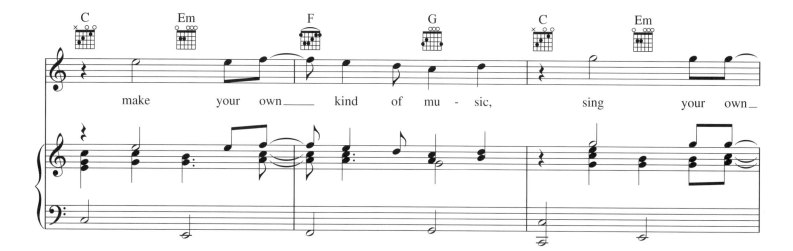

make your own _____ kind of mu - sic, sing your own _____

_____ spe - cial song. _____ Make your own _____ kind of mu - sic

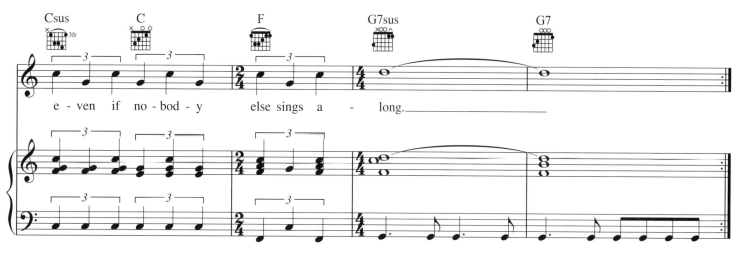

e - ven if no - bod - y else sings a - long. _____

So if you can - not take __ my hand, __

and if you must __ be go - in',

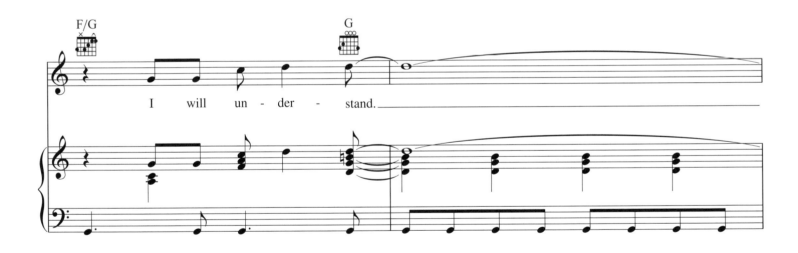

I will un - der - stand. ____

You got - ta

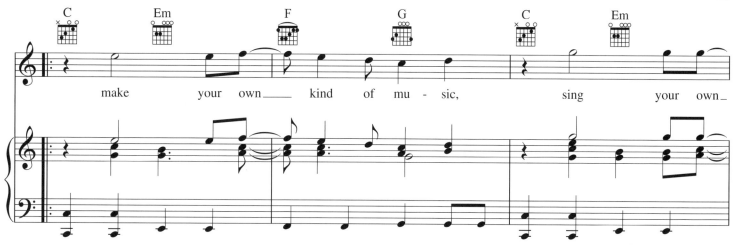

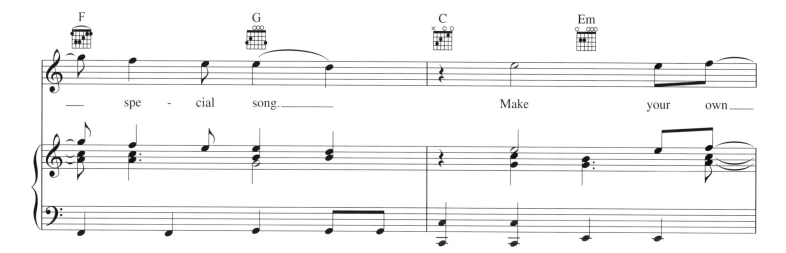

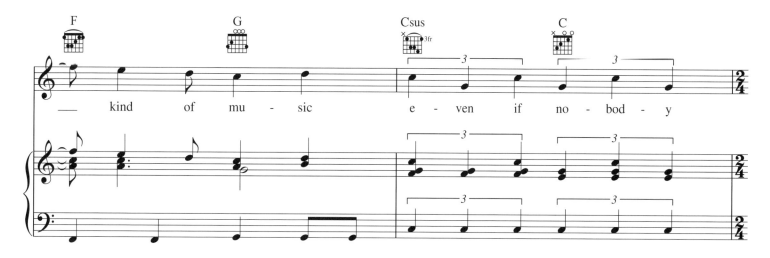

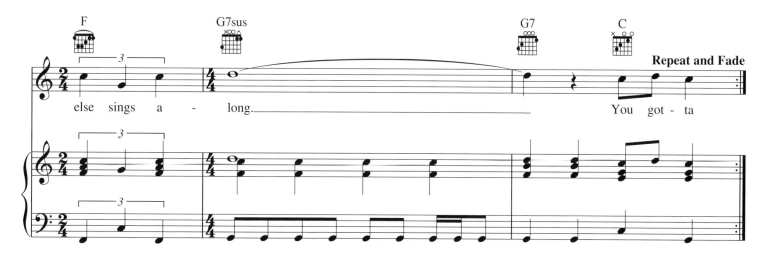

NEVER GONNA LET YOU GO

Words and Music by BARRY MANN
and CYNTHIA WEIL

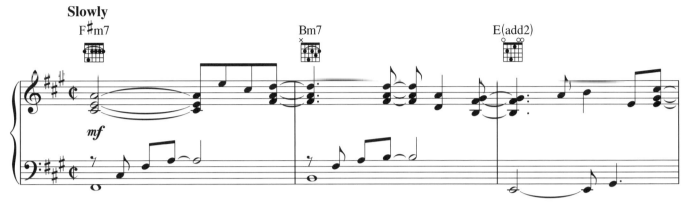

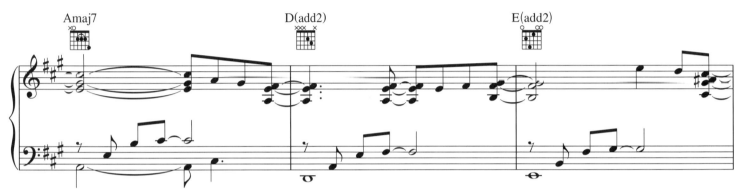

I was as wrong
Look - ing back, now

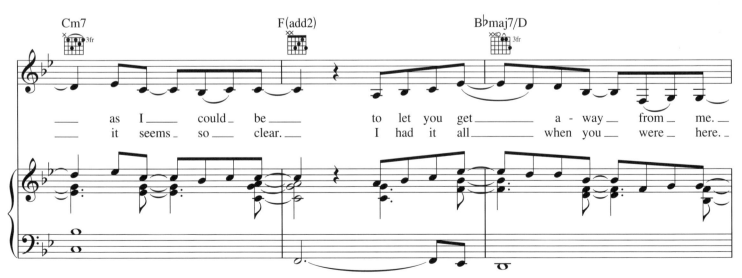

as I could be to let you get a - way from me.
it seems so clear. I had it all when you were here.

I'll re-gret_____ that__ move__ for as long as I'm liv-in'._____
Oh, you gave_____ it__ all__ and I took it for grant-ed._____

But now that I've come_____ to see___ the light,_____
But if there's some feel - ing left___ in you,_____

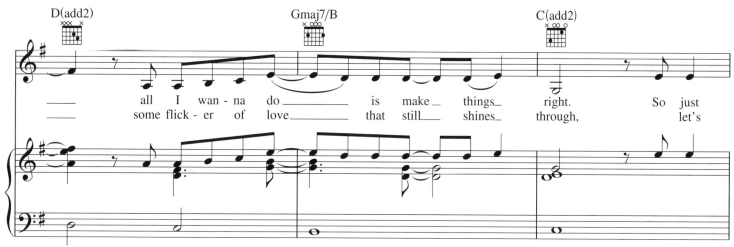

all I wan-na do_____ is make__ things__ right. So just
some flick-er of love_____ that still__ shines__ through, let's

say__ the word_____ and tell me that I'm__ for-giv - en. And
talk__ it out.___ Let's talk a-bout sec - ond chanc - es. And

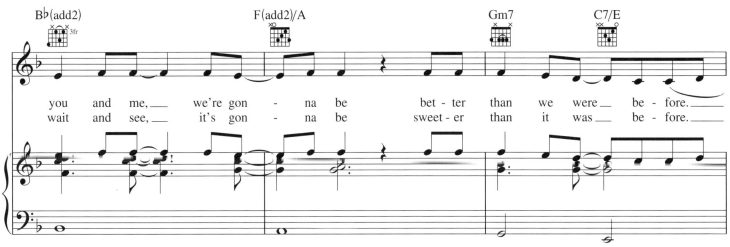

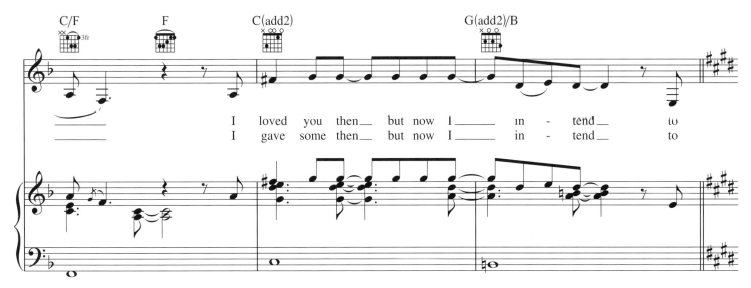

you and me,___ we're gon - na be   bet - ter   than   we   were___ be - fore.___

wait   and   see,___   it's   gon - na   be   sweet - er   than   it   was___   be - fore.

I   loved   you   then___   but   now   I___   in - tend___   to

I   gave   some   then___   but   now   I___   in - tend   to

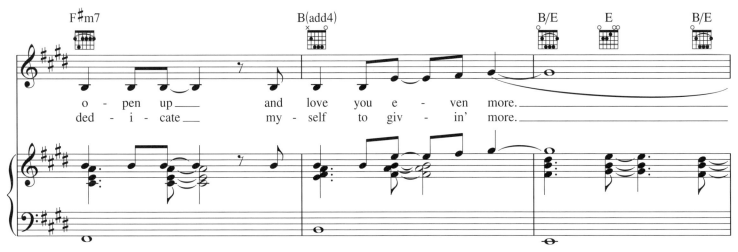

o - pen   up___   and   love   you   e - ven   more.

ded - i - cate___   my - self   to   giv - in'   more.

This   time   you   can___   be   sure.___

This   time   you   can___   be   sure.___   I'm

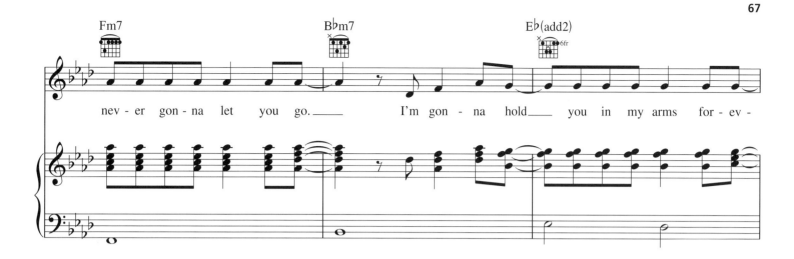

never gonna let you go.____ I'm gon-na hold____ you in my arms for-ev-

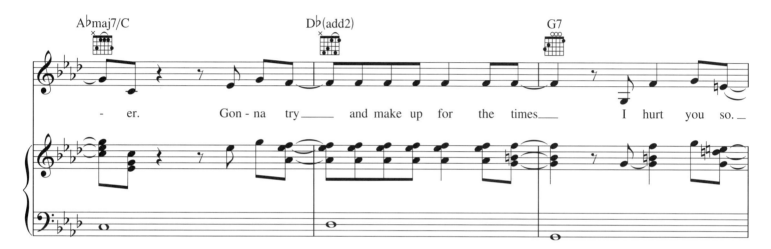

-er. Gon-na try____ and make up for the times____ I hurt you so.____

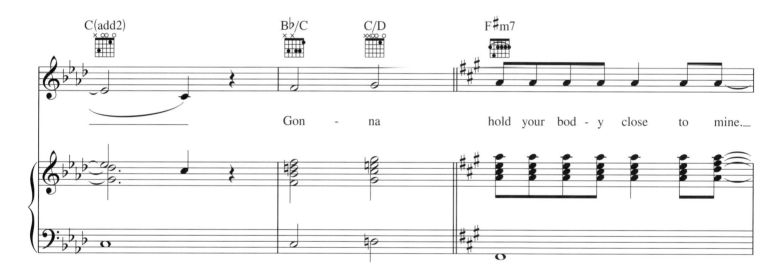

Gon- na hold your bod-y close to mine.____

____ From this day on,____ we're gon-na be to-geth-er. Oh, I

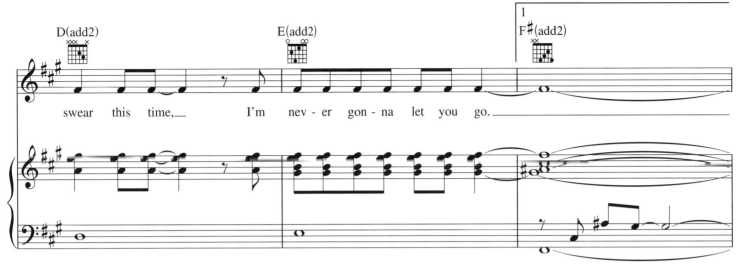

swear this time,___ I'm nev- er gon- na let you go.___

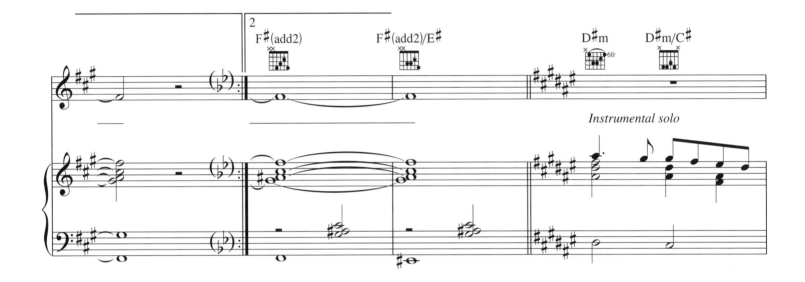

Instrumental solo

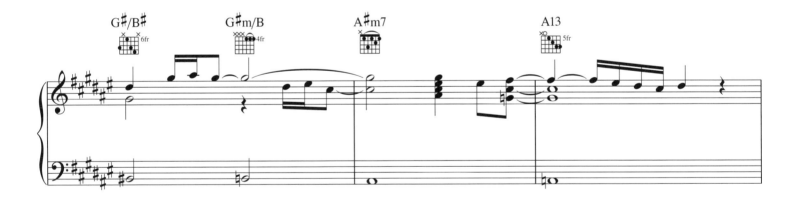

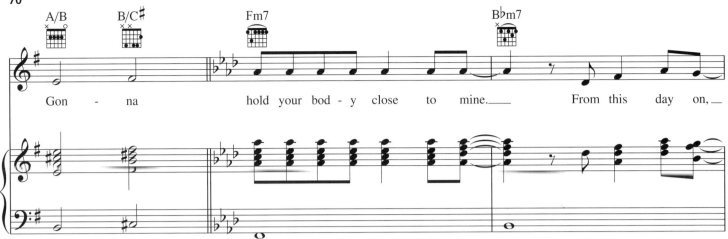

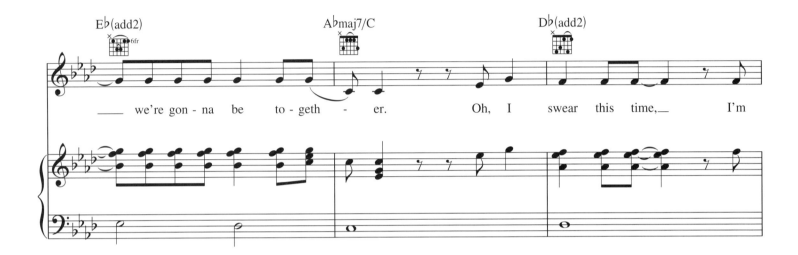

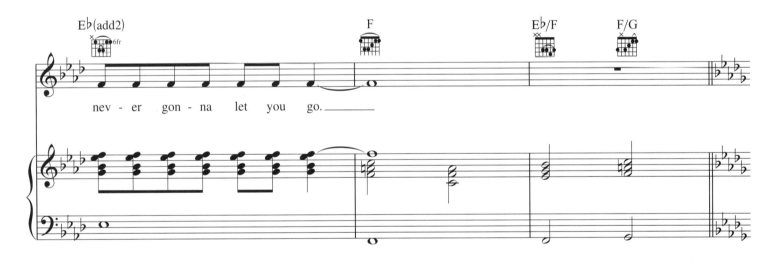

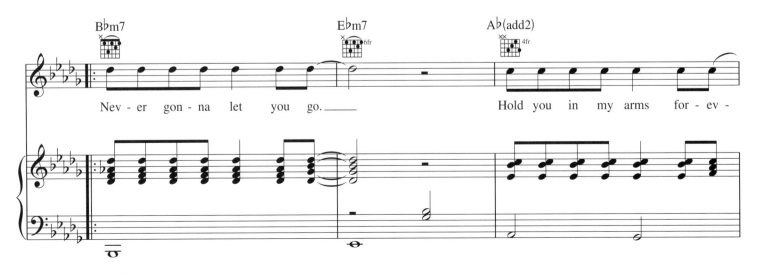

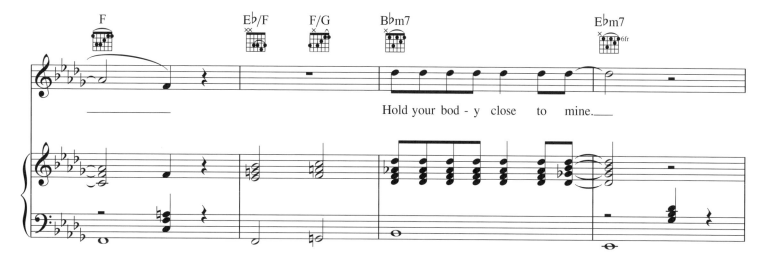

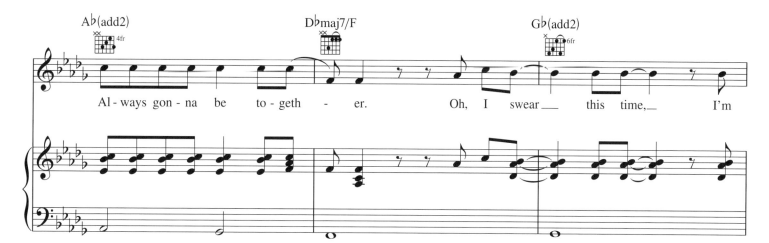

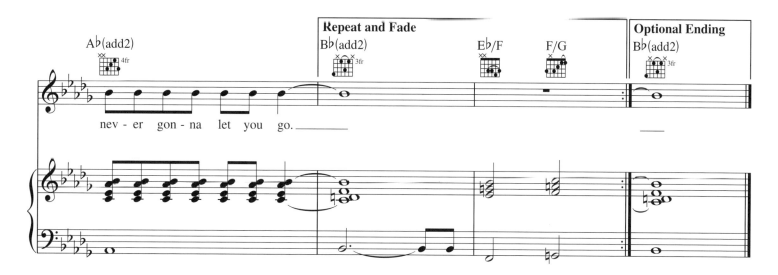

ON BROADWAY

Words and Music by BARRY MANN, CYNTHIA WEIL,
MIKE STOLLER and JERRY LEIBER

Moderately, with a beat

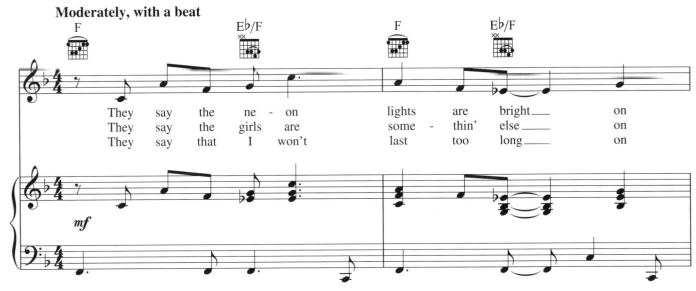

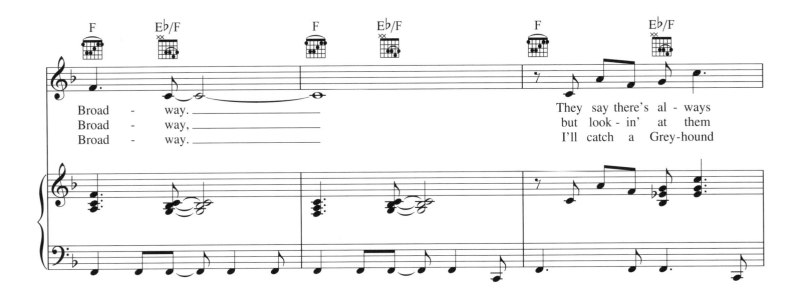

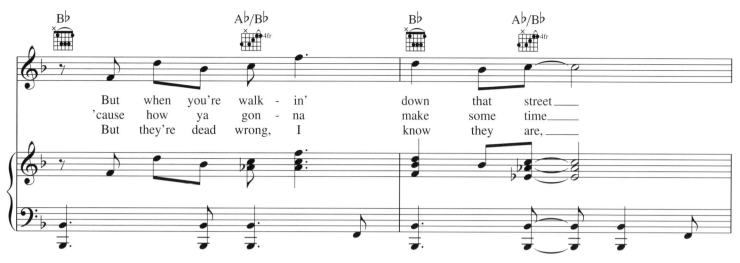

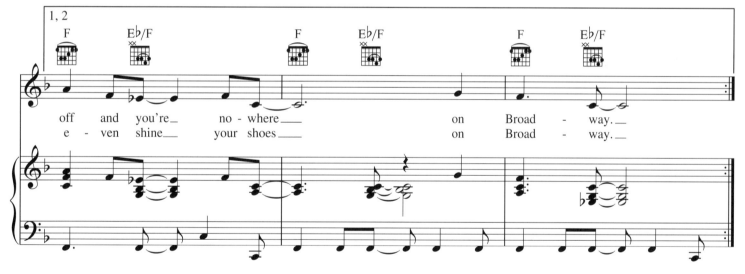

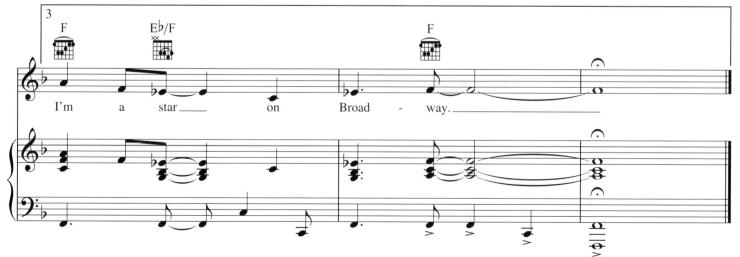

RUNNING WITH THE NIGHT

Words and Music by LIONEL RICHIE
and CYNTHIA WEIL

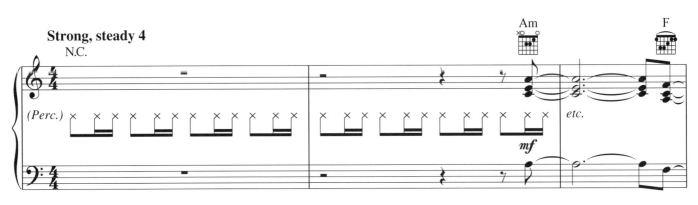

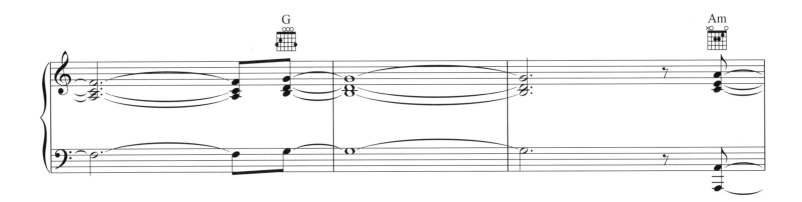

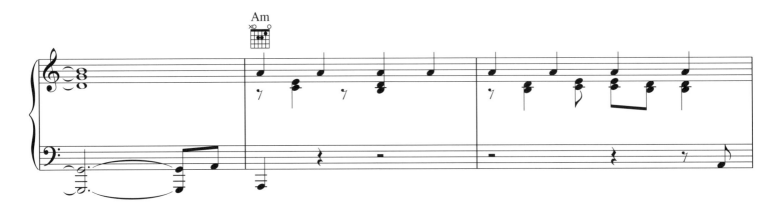

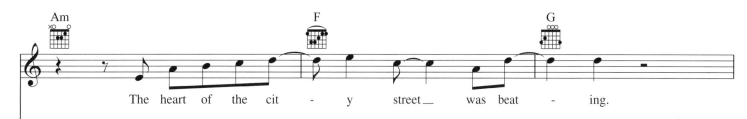

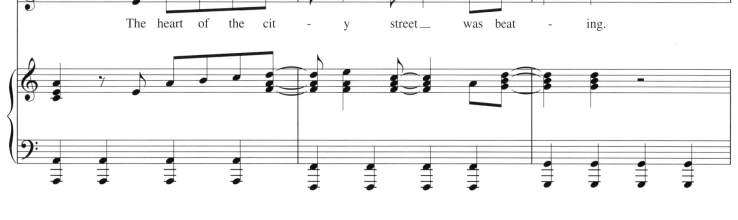

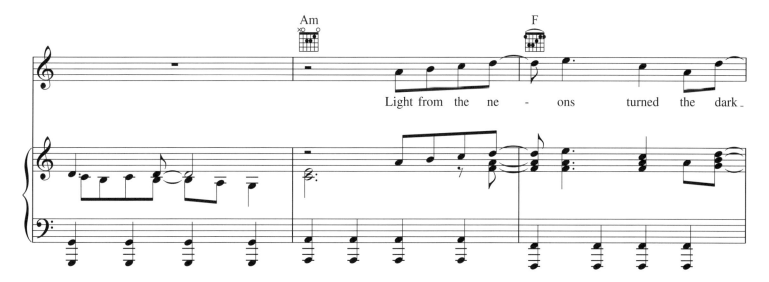

The heart of the cit - y street__ was beat - ing.

Light from the ne - ons turned the dark__

__ to day.__

We were too hot__

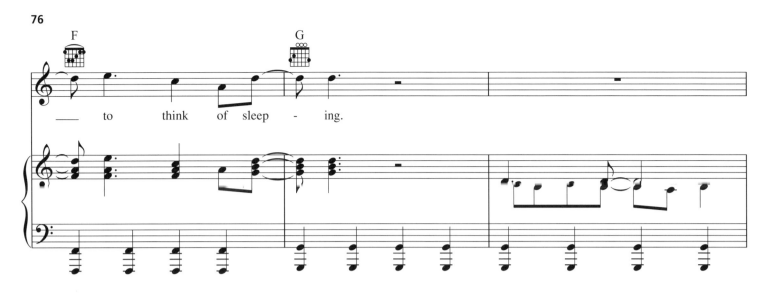

to think of sleep - ing.

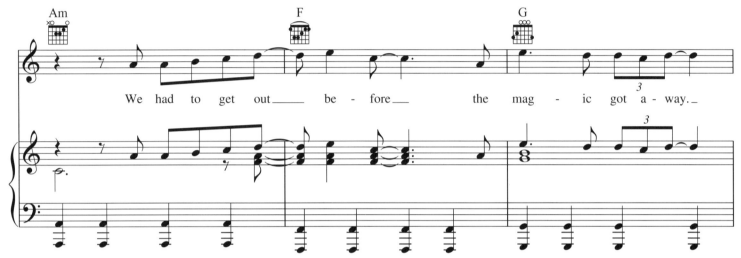

We had to get out___ be - fore___ the mag - ic got a - way.___

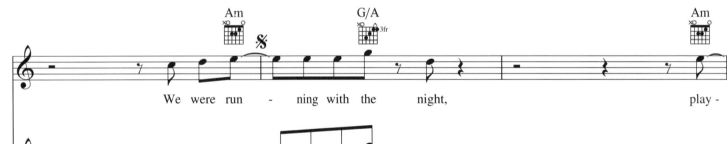

We were run - ning with the night, play -

- ing in the shad - ows, ___ just___ you and I ___

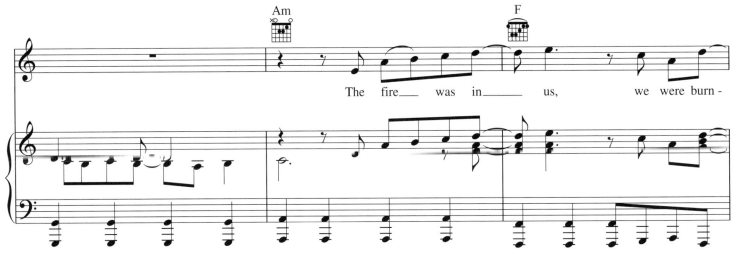

The fire___ was in___ us, we were burn-

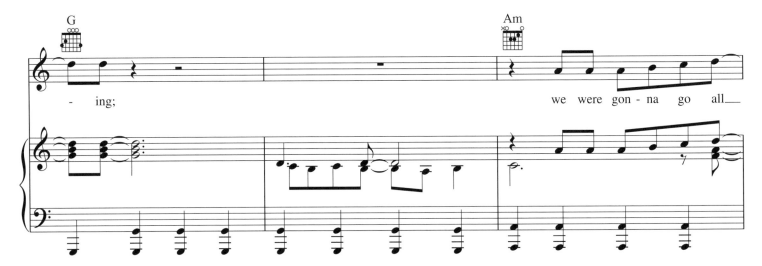

-ing; we were gon-na go all___

D.S. al Coda

___ the way___ and we nev - er had a doubt. We were run-

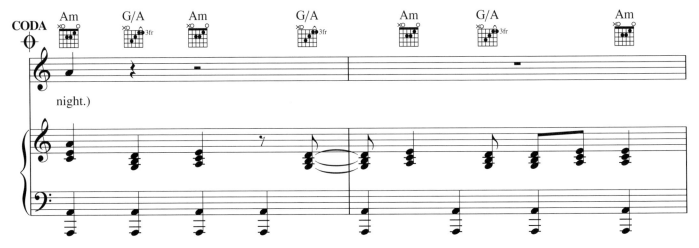

CODA

night.)

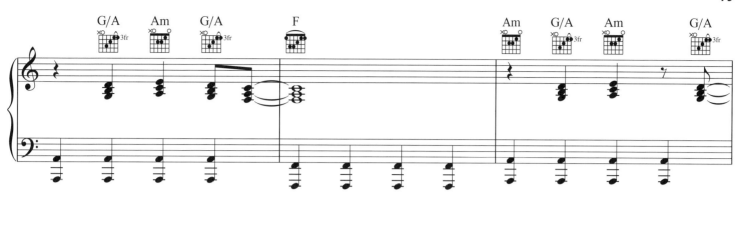

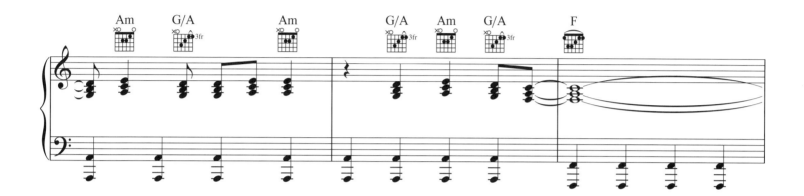

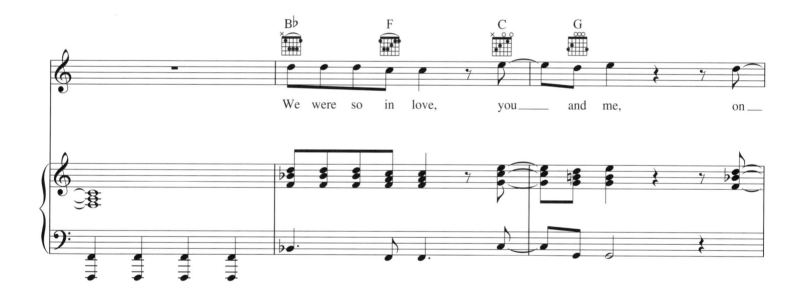

We were so in love, you____ and me, on ____

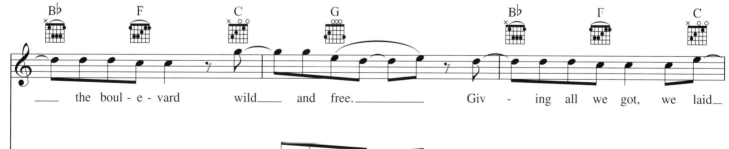

____ the boul - e - vard wild____ and free._____ Giv - ing all we got, we laid__

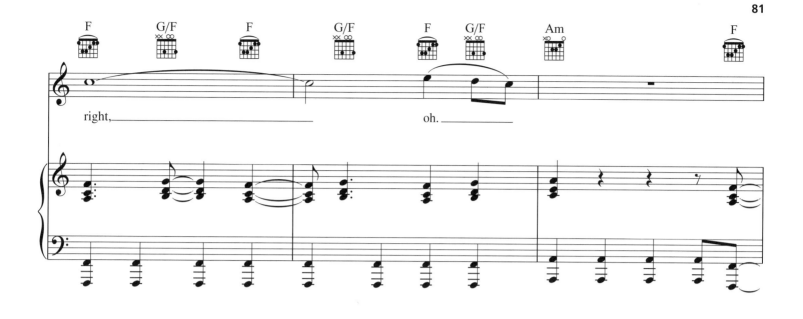

right,_____ oh._____

N.C.

Ooh, _____

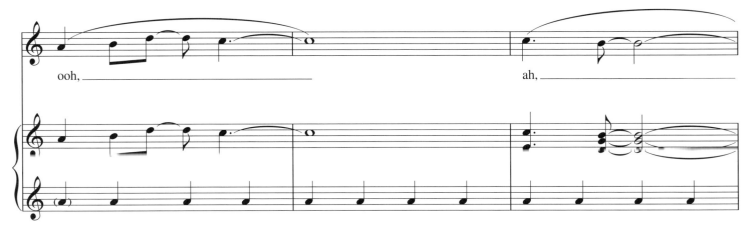

ooh, _____ ah, _____

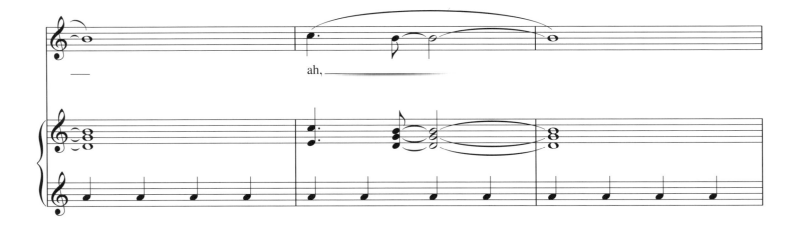

ah, _____ ah, _____

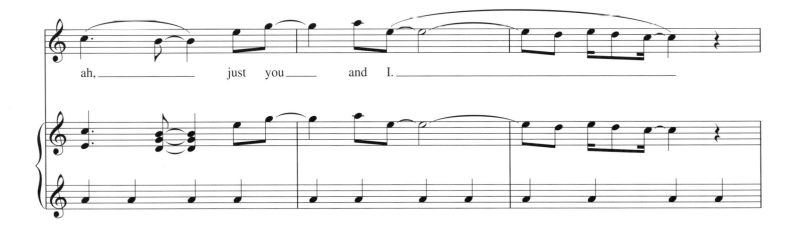

ah, _____ just you _____ and I. _____

Am

We were run -

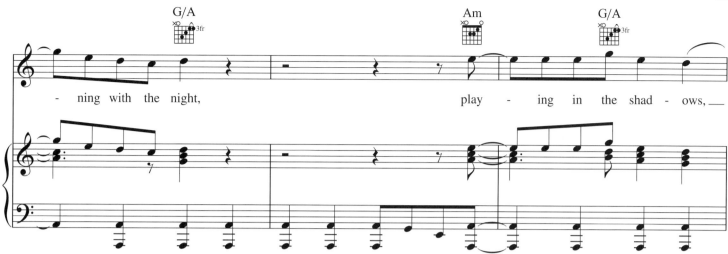

- ning with the night, play - ing in the shad - ows, ___

___ just ___ you and I, ___ girl, it was so right. ___

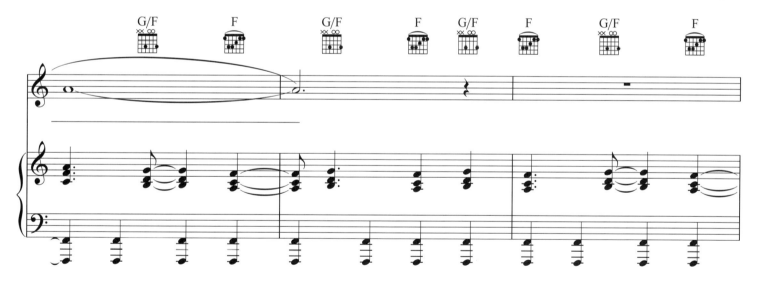

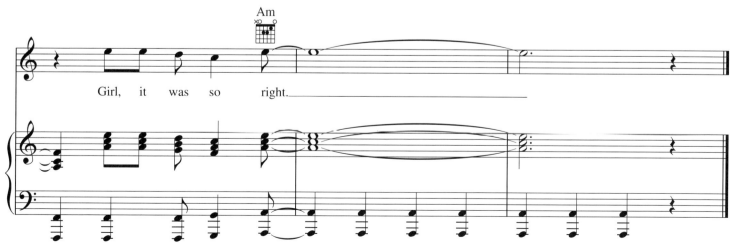

Girl, it was so right. ___

SOMEWHERE OUT THERE

from AN AMERICAN TAIL

Music by BARRY MANN and JAMES HORNER
Lyric by CYNTHIA WEIL

Moderately, with expression

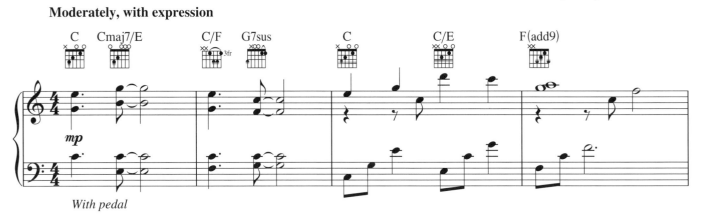

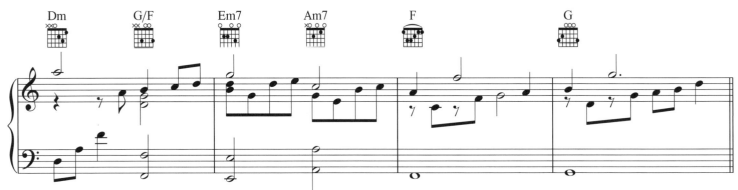

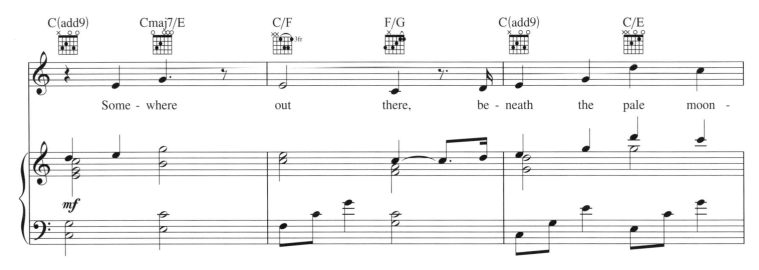

Some - where out there, be - neath the pale moon -

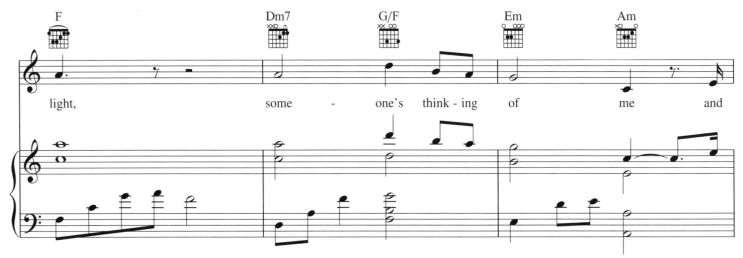

light, some - one's think - ing of me and

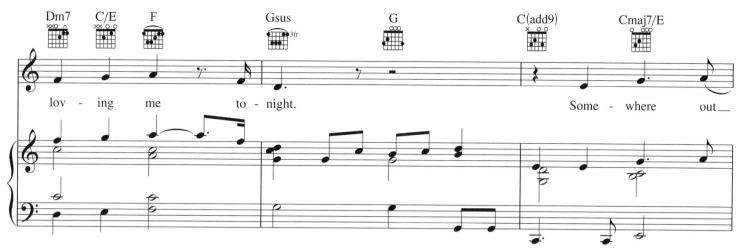

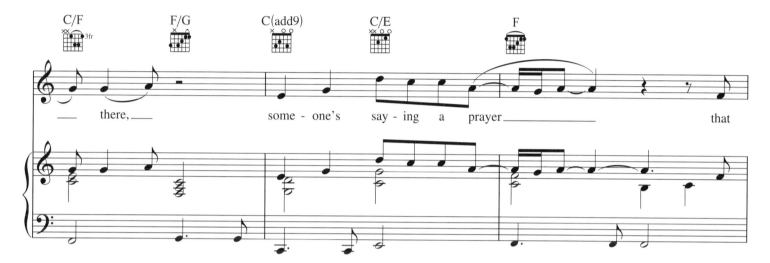

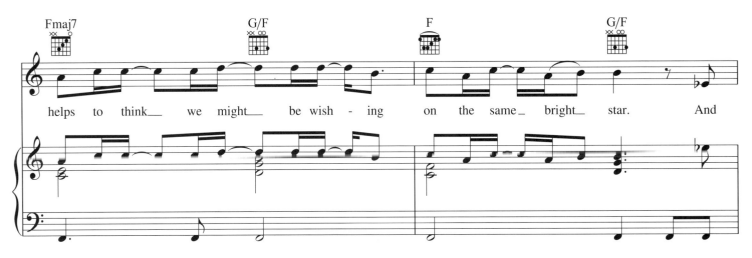

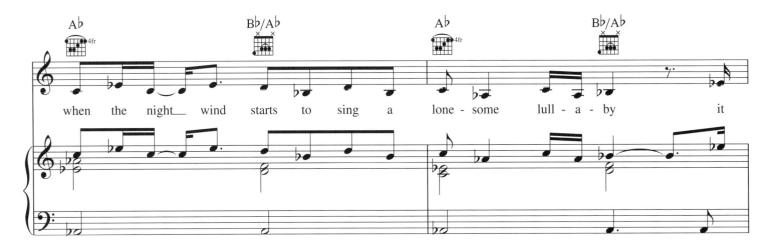

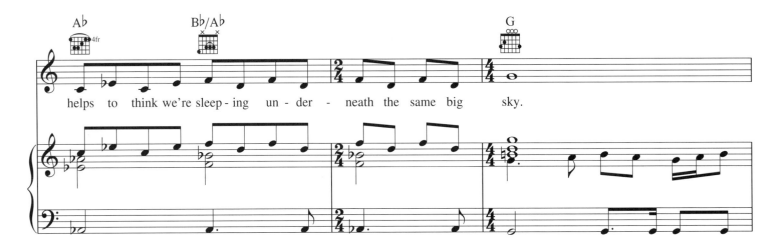

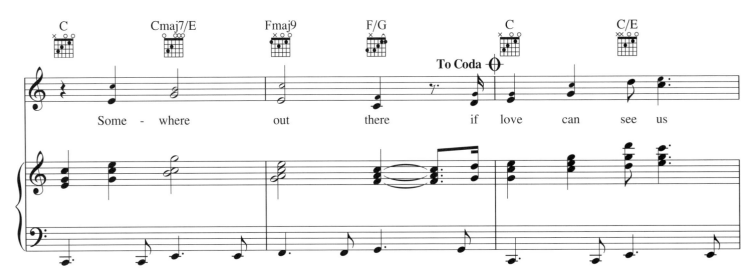

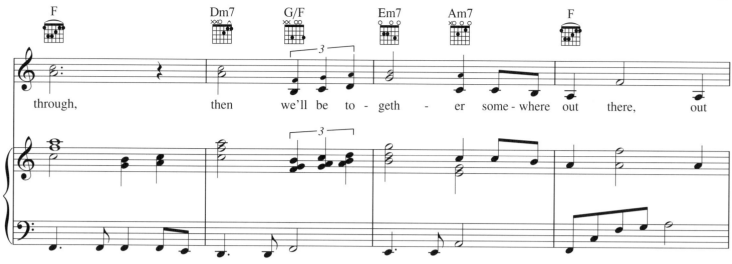

through,   then   we'll be to-geth - er some-where out   there,   out

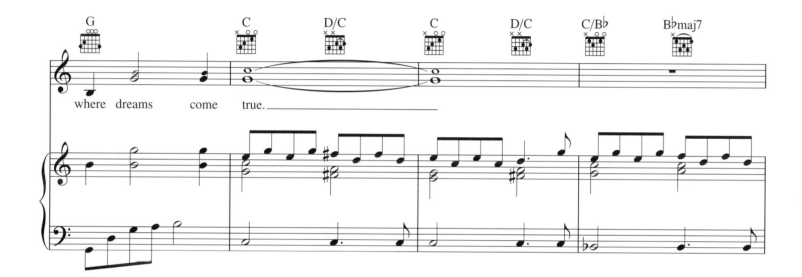

where dreams   come   true._____

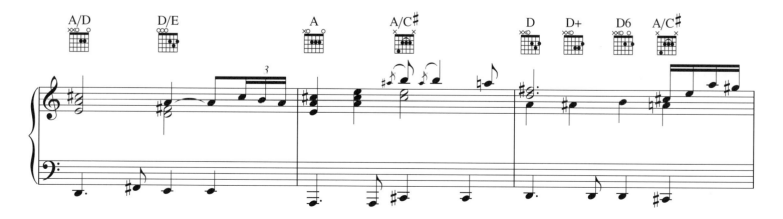

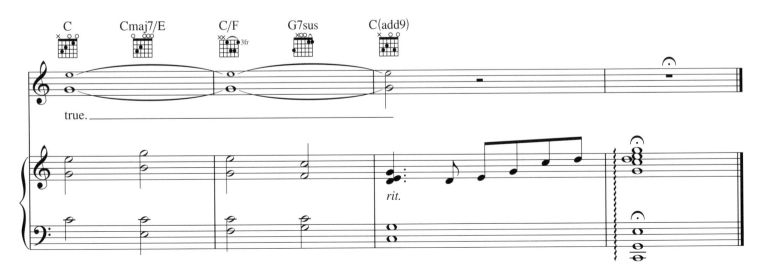

UPTOWN

Words and Music by BARRY MANN
and CYNTHIA WEIL

(You're My)
SOUL AND INSPIRATION

Words and Music by BARRY MANN
and CYNTHIA WEIL

Moderately

Girl,_____ I can't let you do _____ this,
I _____ nev - er had much go - in',

let you walk _____ a - way. _____
but at least _____ I had you. _____

Girl,_____ how can I live through _____ this,
How _____ can you walk out know - in'

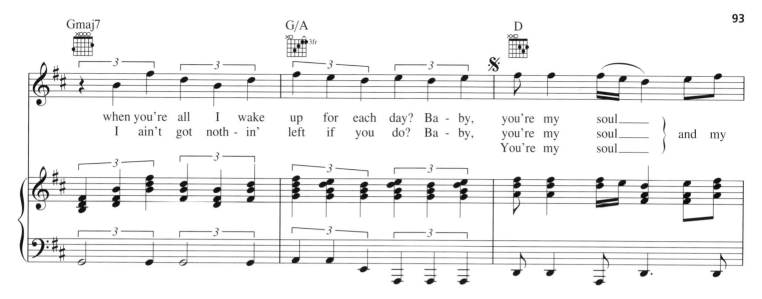

when you're all I wake up for each day? Ba-by, you're my soul____
I ain't got noth-in' left if you do? Ba-by, you're my soul____ } and my
You're my soul____

in - spi - ra - tion. You're all I've got____ to get me by.____

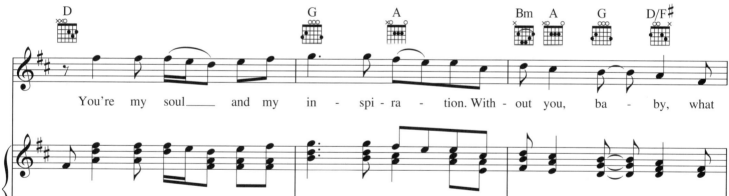

You're my soul____ and my in - spi - ra - tion. With-out you, ba - by, what

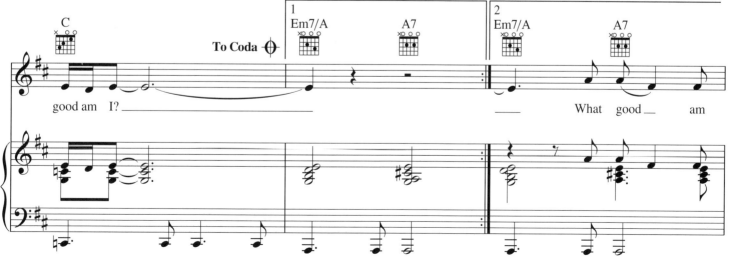

To Coda

good am I?____

What good____ am

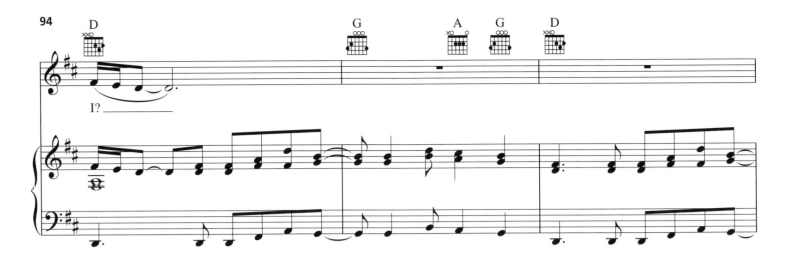

ba - by. _____ If you go,___ it - 'll kill___ me, I swear it, girl.

D.S. al Coda

I just can't bear ___ it.

CODA

___ What good am I? ___

You're my soul___ and my in - spi - ra - tion.

Repeat and Fade

You're all I need ___ to get me by. _____

THROUGH THE FIRE

Music by DAVID FOSTER and TOM KEANE
Lyric by CYNTHIA WEIL

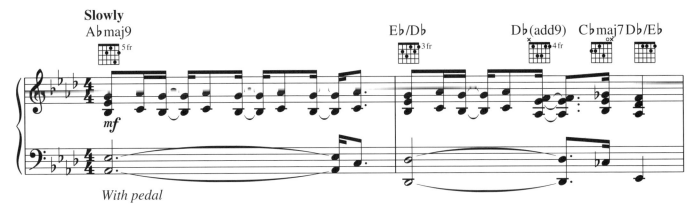

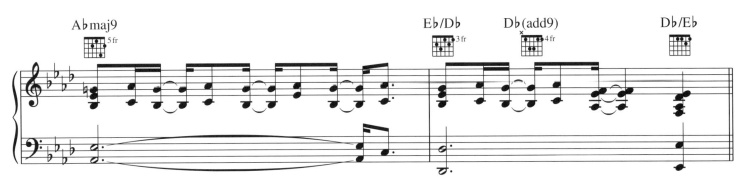

I look in your eyes and I ___ can see you've loved so dan - g'rous -
I know you're a - fraid of what ___ you feel; you still need time ___ to

ly. ___ You're not trust - in' your heart to an - y - one. ___ You tell me you're gon - na play ___ it
heal. ___ But I can help if you'll on - ly let me try. ___ You touched me and some - thing in ___ me

smart; we're through be - fore __ we start. But I be - lieve __ that we've
knew what I could have __ with you. Now I'm not read - y to

on - ly just be - gun. When it's this good, there's no say-in' no.
kiss that dream good-bye. When it's this sweet, there's no say-in' no.

I want you so; I'm read - y to go:
I need you so; I'm read - y to go:

Through the fire, __

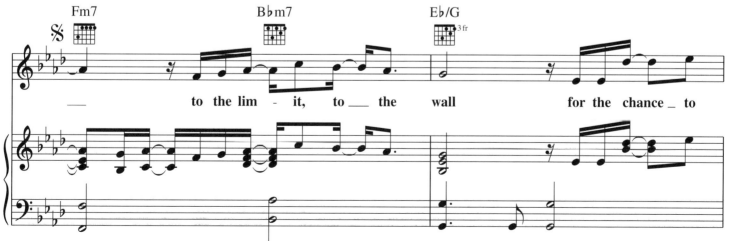

__ to the lim - it, to __ the wall for the chance __ to

WE GOTTA GET OUT OF THIS PLACE

Words and Music by BARRY MANN
and CYNTHIA WEIL

WHO PUT THE BOMP
(In the Bomp Ba Bomp Ba Bomp)

Words and Music by BARRY MANN
and GERRY GOFFIN

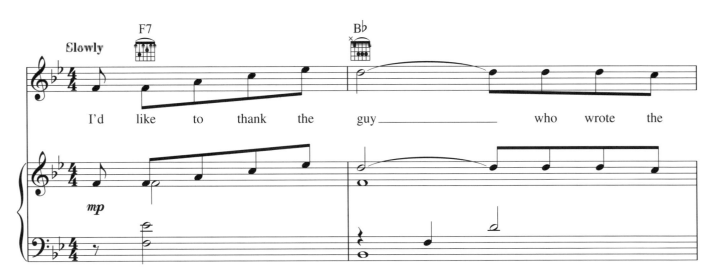

I'd like to thank the guy _____ who wrote the

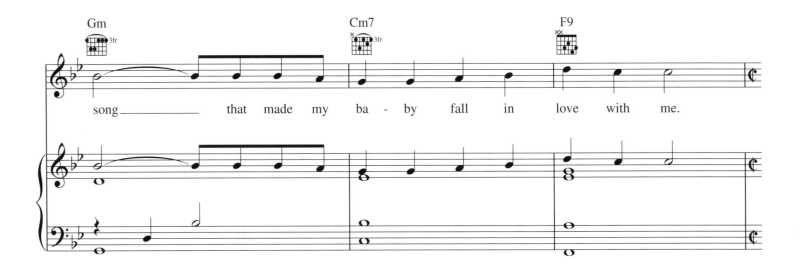

song _____ that made my ba-by fall in love with me.

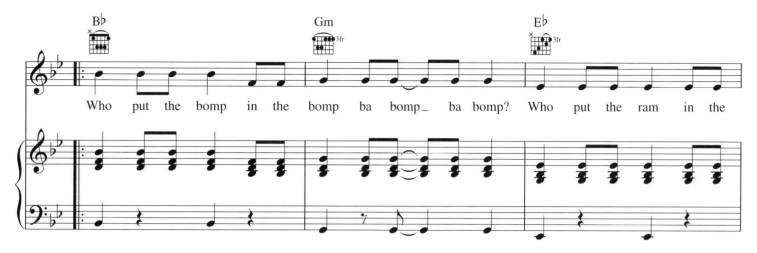

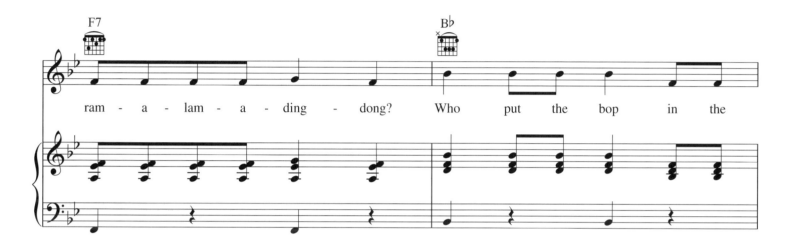

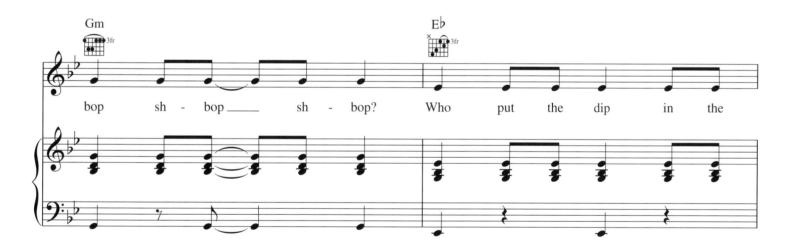

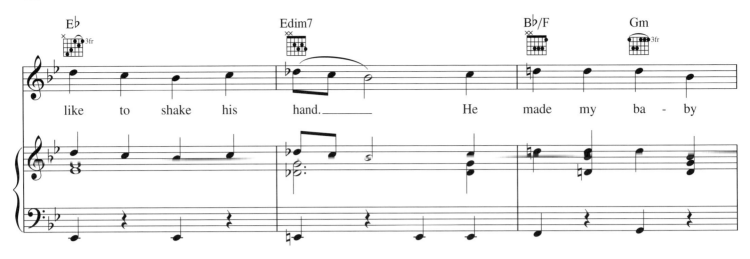

like to shake his hand._____ He made my ba - by

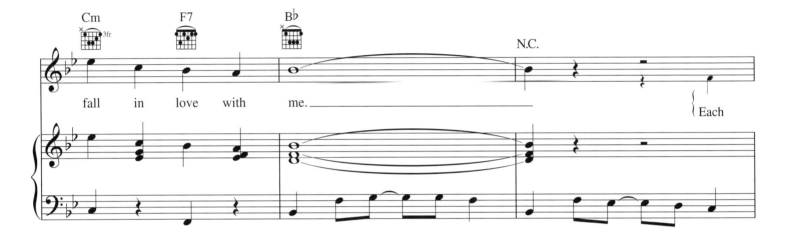

fall in love with me._____ {Each

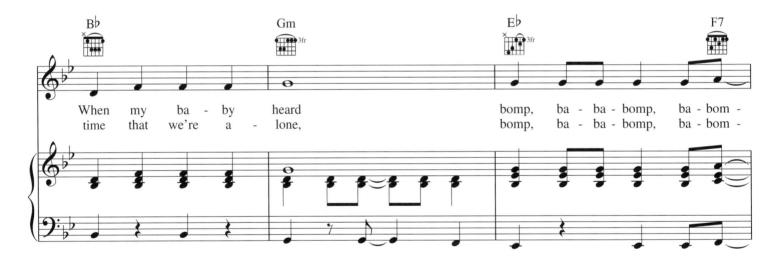

When my ba - by heard   bomp, ba - ba - bomp, ba - bom -
time that we're a - lone,   bomp, ba - ba - bomp, ba - bom -

- ba - bomp - bomp,   ev - 'ry word went   right in - to her
- ba - bomp - bomp,   sets my ba - by's   heart   all a -

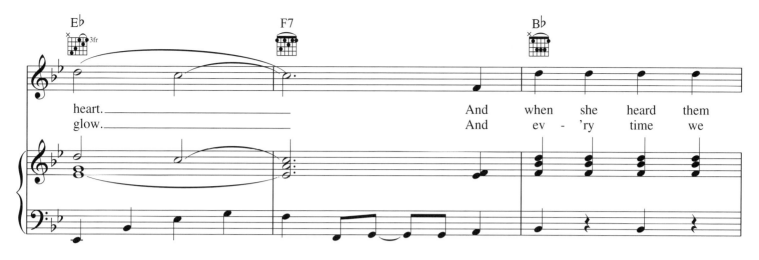

heart._____
glow._____

And when she heard them
And ev - 'ry heard time we

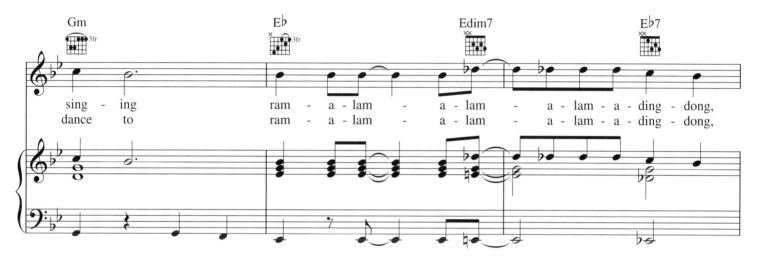

sing - ing ram - a - lam - a - lam - a - lam - a - ding - dong,
dance to ram - a - lam - a - lam - a - lam - a - ding - dong,

she said we'd nev - er have to part._____
she al - ways says she loves me

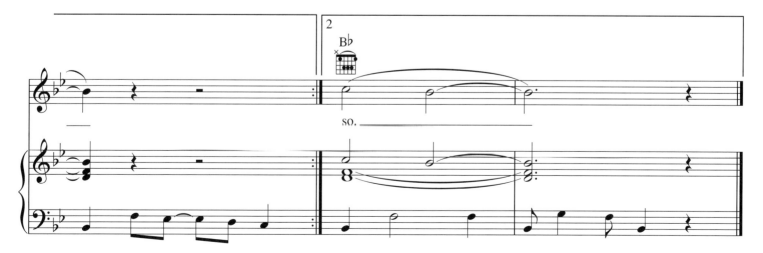

so._____

YOU'VE LOST THAT LOVIN' FEELIN'

Words and Music by BARRY MANN,
CYNTHIA WEIL and PHIL SPECTOR

You nev-er

close your eyes __ an-y-more when I kiss your lips. _____
wel-come look __ in your eyes when I reach for you. _____

And there's no ten-der-ness __ like be-fore in your fin-ger-tips. __
And, girl, you're start-ing to __ crit-i-cize lit-tle things __ I do. __

gone, gone, gone, whoa oh oh oh.

Now, there's no

Ba - by, ba - by, I'd get down on my knees for you.

If that would make you love me like you used to

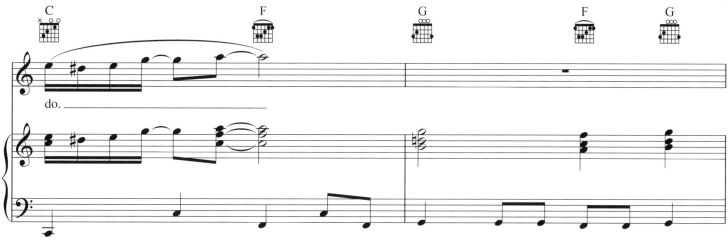

do.

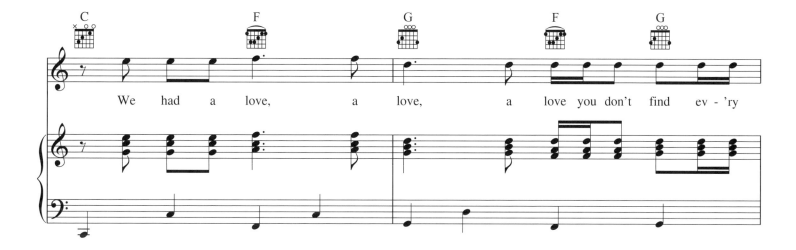

We had a love, a love, a love you don't find ev - 'ry

day. So don't, don't,

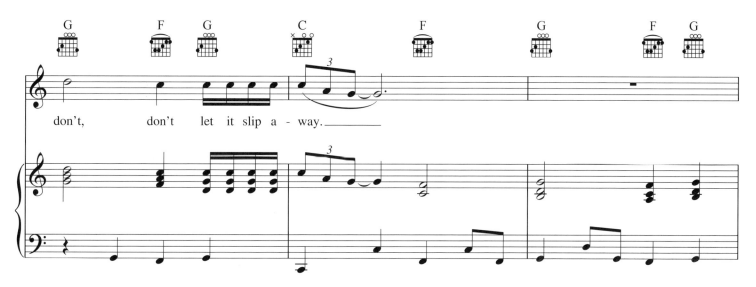

don't, don't let it slip a - way.

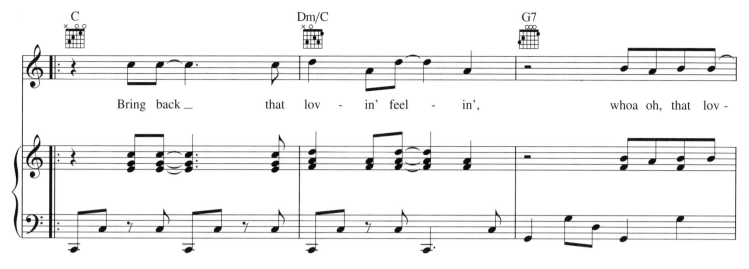

Bring back ___ that lov - in' feel - in', whoa oh, that lov -

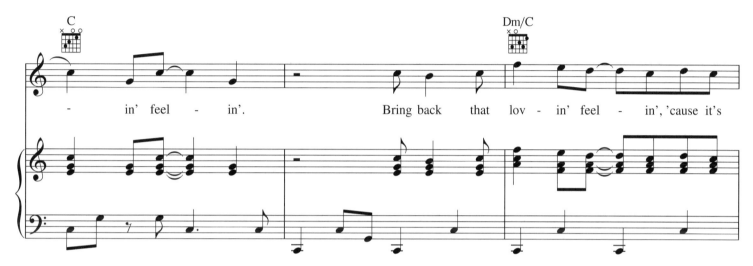

- in' feel - in'. Bring back that lov - in' feel - in', 'cause it's

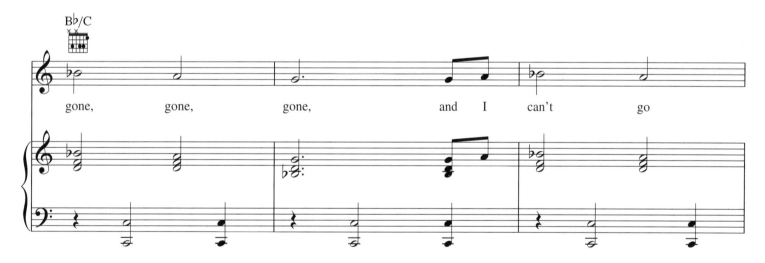

gone, gone, gone, and I can't go

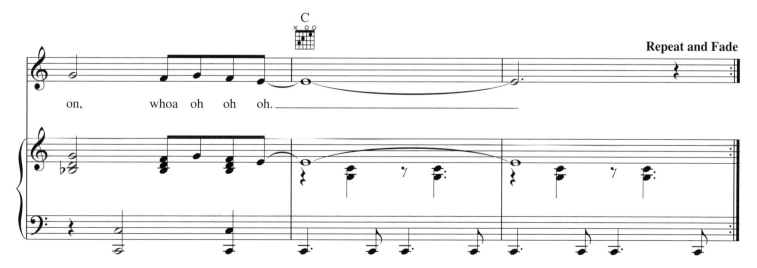

Repeat and Fade

on, whoa oh oh oh. ___

WALKING IN THE RAIN

Words and Music by BARRY MANN,
PHIL SPECTOR and CYNTHIA WEIL

Rock Ballad, not too slow

I want ___ him   and I   need ___ him.
near ___ me,   I'll   kiss ___ him.

And   some-day,   some way,   whoa, _____ I'll
And   when he   leaves me,   whoa, _____ I'll

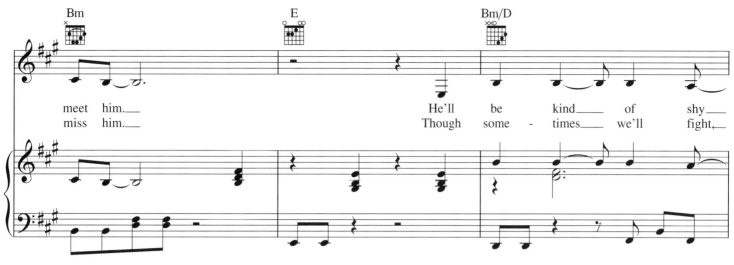

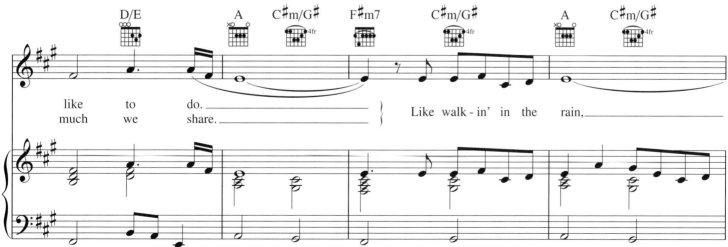

and wish- in' on the stars up a - bove, ___ and be - ing so

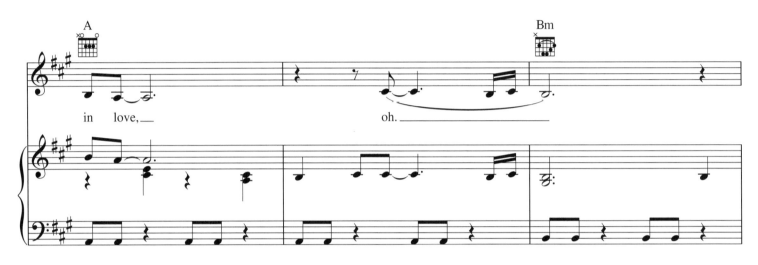

in love, ___ oh. ___

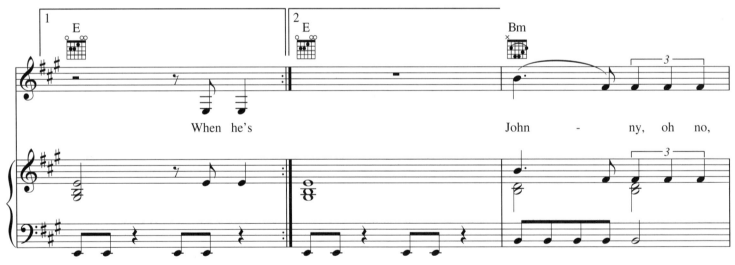

When he's

John - ny, oh no,

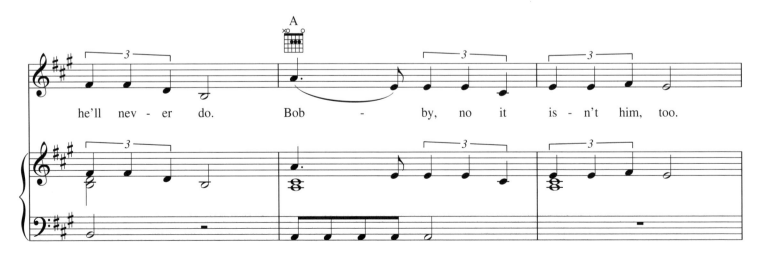

he'll nev - er do. Bob - by, no it is - n't him, too.

They would nev - er, no, they'd nev - er, nev - er,

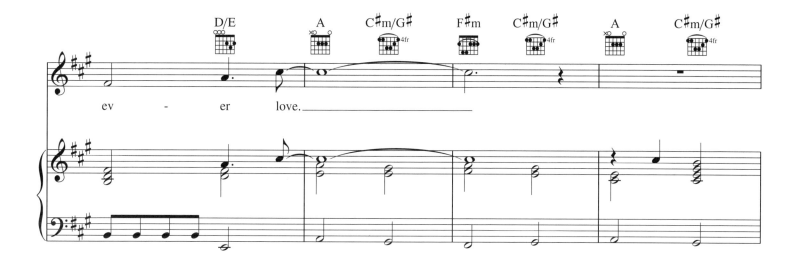

ev - er love._____

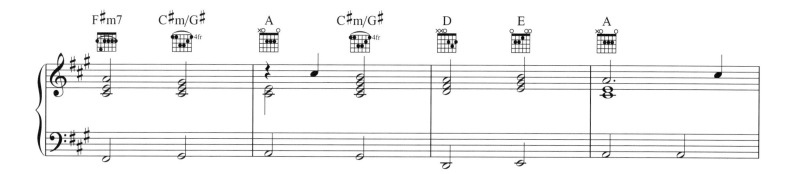

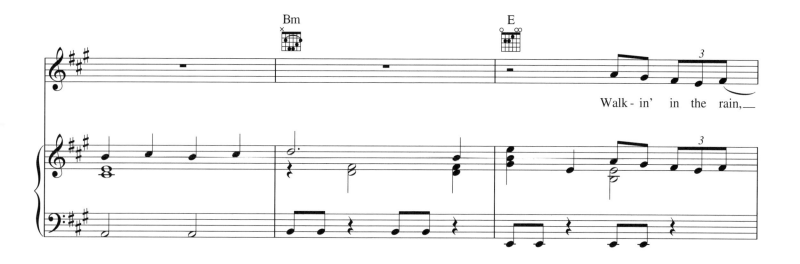

Walk - in' in the rain,__

and talk-ing in the rain,

___ and wish-ing on the stars ___ a - bove, ___ and be-ing so

in love. ___ Oh, oh, ___ oh, ___

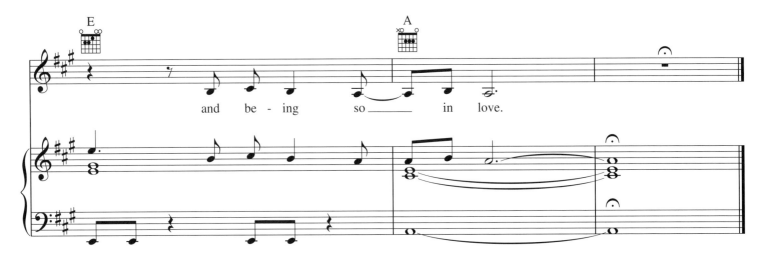

and be - ing so ___ in love.